John Mic

Signatures

DAN O'NEILL

John Michael Talbot
Signatures

The Story of
John Michael Talbot

Troubadour For The Lord Contact Information:
Troubadour For The Lord
350 CR 248 / Berryville, AR 72631
(479) 253-0256 Fax: (479) 253-0260

ISBN 1-883803-10-1

Printed in the United States of America
10   9   8   7   6   5   4   3   2   1

Cover design by Peter Davidson
Cover photo by Rick Ims
Book design by Ric Simenson

*This book is dedicated to
The Brothers and Sisters of Charity,
the Brothers and Sisters of Charity Domestic,
and to the memory of Dick and Jamie Talbot,
loving parents of John Michael Talbot*

Acknowledgement

I wish to acknowledge John Michael Talbot for his courage and candor in sharing his life through this book. Additionally, deep gratitude must be expressed to John Michael and his community for supporting the global humanitarian mission of Mercy Corps, which exists to alleviate suffering, poverty and oppression by helping people build secure, productive and just communities. www.MercyCorps.Org

— Dan O'Neill

Contents

Preface

The troubadours were itinerant lyric poets and musicians who flourished in Europe from the eleventh through the thirteenth century. They wandered throughout the continent, particularly in southern France, northern Italy, and western Spain. Their rhymes were usually love songs, and most of these medieval minstrels composed their own material. It was not uncommon for them to have noble blood in their veins-they were the upper class, establishment dropouts of their era.

Giovanni Francesco Bernardone was just such a person. He was born the son of a wealthy cloth merchant in the Italian town of Assisi in about 1182. Francis, as he was later to be called, opted out of the status quo as the result of a profound religious conversion experience. Donning a ragged cloak of sackcloth belted with a length of rope, he proceeded to incite a peaceful "overthrow" of Europe in a gentle revolution of love. The intriguing tales of Saint Francis of Assisi have filled the hearts and imaginations of men for nearly eight hundred years and have become incarnate in the lives and works of worldwide movement, the Order of Friars Minor, or the Franciscans, in all its diverse forms and expressions.

Francis also symbolizes a return to all the best of the entire monastic tradition, while constantly going forward through the Gospel of Jesus Christ. The Desert Fathers, the hermits and community dwellers, the pilgrims and the penitents, even the Hindu Sannyasin and Buddhist mendicants are all somehow included and motivated further forward in the life and example of St. Francis.

Today Saint Francis's spiritual revival continues, not only within the traditional ranks of lay and religious Franciscans, but in a growing atmosphere of social awakening, ecumenical dialogue, and international spiritual renewal. A growing number of Christian pilgrims are walking in the footsteps of a truly legendary figure, committing themselves to the radical Gospel expression of love as exemplified by the life of Saint Francis, one of our Lord's most dynamic and colorful disciples. The interfaith meetings called by Pope John Paul II symbolize an even further appeal of the saint today.

One such individual is John Michael Talbot, a former country-rock musician, who captures the true spirit of Franciscan spirituality; from his dark brown habit to his inspiring music, he bears the unmistakable marks of a modern-day troubadour and monastic mystic. Through a new expression of monastic spirituality, he has offered up his entire life and prodigious talent to God. His story will inspire you.

— Dan O'Neill

John Michael Talbot
Signatures

A Musical Inheritance

It was March 27, 1982. I landed at the Sacramento airport, hastily rented a car, and smiled to myself as I drove to Saint Ignatius Catholic Church. I'll be early, I thought, with the certainty of one who likes compulsive, detailed planning. Wrong. As I turned into the expansive church parking lot there was not a slot to be found, and a dozen other drivers were cruising for spaces. My first surprise at a John Michael Talbot concert was being unable to find a parking place, even though I had arrived ninety minutes early.

As the late-afternoon Mass concluded at Saint Ignatius, a swelling crowd clamored at several entrances in eager anticipation. Unlike other religious concerts I had attended, this one was attracting an audience much more diverse than the predictably youthful following of most contemporary Christian performers. Small children, teens, collegiates, married couples and senior citizens created a kind of extended-family atmosphere, complete with a generous sprinkling of priests and nuns who speckled the crowd with black-and-white habits and clerical collars. I began to sense a contagious quality of expectation and excitement.

Tucked discreetly away in an adjacent building, John Michael Talbot was directing the final rehearsal with the one hundred-voice choir. Of course, I eavesdropped. Crouching in a corner I observed John as he orchestrated several of the evening's upcoming numbers. A tenor leaned over and whispered nervously in my ear, "We've been practicing a whole year for this single night!" Now, that's commitment—no wonder they sounded so good.

As the big moment approached, John led the singers in a hushed, brief prayer. "Lord Jesus, lead us, direct us, minister through us in the creative, spontaneous power of Your Holy Spirit. We have worked, now You do Your work. Make us instruments of Your peace. In the name of the Father, the Son, and the Holy Spirit, amen." Now I was fully caught up in the flow of the event. For me, the concert had already begun.

John slung his guitar over his back and shuffled toward me with a grin on his bearded face. "It's about time you caught one of these concerts, Dan. I think you'll really enjoy it." In those days, he looked every inch the Franciscan monk, with the hooded dark-brown habit draped over his tall, lean frame. He fiddled unconsciously with the knotted white rope that traditionally belts the garment of the disciples of Saint Francis and continued, "I have reserved a front-row seat for you."

In my excellent vantage point in the sanctuary of the spacious church, I produced a pen and paper to record my impressions. A full half-hour before the start of the concert, the place was packed—even standing room was gone and hundreds were being turned away at the door. All eyes were riveted on the empty stage when John emerged to test the microphones. Applause burst forth spontaneously. "Testing... testing one, two, testing."

"Oooh!" His voice sounds just like on his records!" a teenage girl squealed. "And he looks even better than on the album jacket." Obviously this guy has dedicated fans, I noted to myself. People even love his sound checks! John joked with those in the first few rows as he tuned his guitar.

As the house lights gradually faded to a dim glow, silence cloaked the hall. The melodious notes of the skillfully played instrument suddenly filled the air and a long, narrow shaft of light pierced the darkness, falling on the robed figure that leaned into the microphone with closed eyes and uplifted face.

"Sing alleluia to the Wonderful Counselor..." the voice drifted through the place like sweet incense. More than eighteen hundred listeners hung on every word, every note, until the song concluded, then roared in unrestrained approval. Flash bulbs and strobes popped by the score.

"I hope you didn't come here this evening to be entertained. I left that business about ten years ago." Smiling, he paused a moment and urged, "Let us enter into the presence of God in song. Saint Augustine said, 'He who sings well, prays twice.'" The throng joined in with enthusiasm in a round of "Sing alleluia". It sounded like heaven—a truly amazing experience.

At the end of the song John paused, rolled up his loose brown sleeves, propped his bare feet on a rung of the stool on which he was perched, and explained, "Singing is really a form of prayer. It demonstrates unity when we all join together in this collective act of prayerful worship. Let's reflect on this as we continue our worship together this evening." He bowed his head in supplication, hands folded.

Silent moments passed. Then his fingers once again danced deftly across the strings of his guitar with expert precision. Melodious songs of praise flowed effortlessly and he captivated the audience through his gentle, endearing manner. He sang "Holy Is His Name," "The Lilies of the Field," and, of course, the timeless "Peace Prayer of Saint Francis."

"In my more contemplative moments I often think of my life as though it were an empty canvas. I visualize Jesus as a master painter. We can become something beautiful—the creative work of his infinitely skilled hands." John launched into "Empty Canvas" from his album *The Painter*, an apparent favorite of many in the audience.

Then, the grand finale—songs from John's best-selling album *The Lord's Supper* complete with the large choir. "We Shall Stand Forgiven" was followed by "Glory to God in the Highest," at which point the place exploded with high praise and boundless, jubilant worship. The sanctuary was electrified by the sound of nearly two thousand voices. I had never seen anything quite like this—it was almost Pentecostal, yet somehow tempered by Catholic restraint and order.

John spoke with a kind of hushed, firm confidence. "You know, we would all represent an incredible force for peace if we would just unite and take our faith seriously. The revolution must begin inside in our hearts! I am speaking of a gentle revolution, free as the wind—you can't see it, but this awesome energy is all around us in the power of the Spirit."

Finally, at John's request we stood and joined hands, singing the Lord's Prayer. I later wrote in my journal that this was a "salient moment of pure spiritual vitality, made tangible by the human linkage of hands and hearts."

Most of the throng filed out of the church on a spiritual high, while a remaining hundred or so rushed the stage, hoping for a photo, an autograph, or perhaps a word or two with the Franciscan brother who had had such immense impact that evening. It took me more than an hour to extricate John from the place.

"Well, what do you think? Did it go okay? How bout the choir, did their voices project?" John asked anxiously, seemingly unaware of his great success. "All I want is to glorify God, and follow Jesus."

"I would say you succeeded, brother," I replied.

Who is John Michael Talbot? Many have followed the

singer's career for three decades. To some, he was the young banjo player at an Indiana state fair; to others a balladeer singing songs of love. For an entire generation of early-seventies dropouts, radicals, and students, John sang mellow songs of protest and idealism, dreaming of alternatives for a better world. To the youthful evangelical Christians of the Jesus movement, John was a reformed recording star who had chosen the straight and narrow, gently rocking their souls with contemporary Christian musical messages. Finally, there is a rapidly expanding group for whom John is a Catholic minstrel, softly singing of the ancient apostolic faith, beckoning those who have ears to hear to return to the roots of their spiritual heritage.

Is he a contemporary musician or a religious leader, a layperson or monk, rich or poor, a hermit or community founder, a Franciscan or founder of a new monastic community, a charismatic or contemplative, an orthodox Roman Catholic or an ecumenical and interfaith explorer and pioneer? All of these questions present themselves to anyone taking more than just a superficial look at the man.

There are almost as many different images of Talbot as there are listeners of his music. Some have wondered which of John's many diverse expressions is the real one. The answer can only be, all of them—in the sense that we all are who we are today because of where we have been yesterday. John is no exception to this rule. His life has been a process and a pilgrimage, an intriguing personal journey evolving toward an increasingly powerful statement of the Gospel of Christ.

In an era of heightened interest in our cultural and spiritual roots, John's prophetic, lyrical call to orthodoxy and liturgical worship are at the forefront of today's renewal movement. Certainly there are those who see him as a throwback to medievalism—an anachronism robed in sackcloth. There are others, however, who see him as a sign of things to come—the beginning of a powerful new lay movement in the church, and perhaps even in society at large.

In this book we will look at the life of a musician who at the age of fourteen was already touring America as a professional musician, and now, over three decades later, is commanding sold-out concerts and huge record sales with his stunningly simple expression of monastic spirituality. This book is not a biography as much as it is an unfinished narrative about a troubadour—a troubadour working tirelessly in the service of the Lord.

Where did it start? What were the beginnings of this journey and this dream? In any attempt to observe the life flow of a person, it is essential to first focus on the historical background of the individual.

John's mother was Jamie Margaret Talbot, now buried beside her husband on the grounds of Little Portion Hermitage, near Eureka Springs, Arkansas. Her earliest recollections were of her father, the late Reverend James Cochran, an itinerant singing Methodist minister who covered a lot of ground preaching in his home state of Oklahoma. Most of the men in her family were traveling preachers, including Jamie's grandfather, seven uncles, and brothers.

For much of her life, she endured nagging illness. During one of her childhood attacks, a neighbor made an urgent house call. Not only did she have words of comfort, encouragement, and prayer, but she baptized the Methodist minister's child on the spot. The neighbor, it turned out, was a Catholic.

At the time this curious event left no discernible impression on little Jamie, although she did recover fully from her illness. It was only much later that the real significance of this sacramental encounter became evident, and ultimately led her on a path that was to change her life forever.

While the devotion of Jamie's father to his calling was apparent, there were elements of her life as a "preacher's kid" (such as the political maneuverings of behind-the-scenes church life) that were to produce in later years a kind of spiritual estrangement from her Christian upbringing. But, as is so often the case with prodigals an eventual homecoming followed her time of spiritual drift and disillusionment.

Jamie married Dick Talbot, a good-natured man with a keen sense of humor. Dick bubbled with enthusiasm and was more than just a little strong-willed.

"Dad was an Army Air Corps man in World War II," John recalls. "He was based in India and flew those big B-24 bombers over 'the hump' into Burma. Actually, he started out as a pilot but he was booted out of pilot training school

John Michael's parents, Jamie and Richard Talbot.

because he was always skipping out to see my mother. They dropped him into navigation school where he was promptly bounced because he persisted in his unauthorized visits to Mom. Next came bombardier training where, you guessed it, he was fingered again, after a military policeman discovered him hiding in the trunk of a buddy's car, heading out to see Mom. His romantic inclinations ultimately got him stuck in the dreaded position of waist gunner, where he was much more open to being hit by rounds from enemy fighter planes. As I think back now, I can still remember Dad gazing skyward more than once, recalling the friends he lost during that long, awful war. He was very fortunate to get through it."

Dick Talbot was a typical man of the World War II generation. He was religious, but very self-reliant. He was a good husband and father. The family went to church a few times a month as good Methodists. Due to his exposure to other religions of the world during the war, he instilled within John a respect for all faiths, especially the Hindu and Buddhist traditions of India where he was stationed, and openness to peoples of every race. He was very personable, and worked in sales and public relations most of his life. After the war he worked for Braniff Airlines, and was on a first name basis with presidents and dignitaries. Yet, there remained something intensely private about him.

Together, Dick and Jamie established their home, first in Kansas City, Missouri, later in Oklahoma City. The first child was Terry; a year later, Tanni came, followed five years after, in Oklahoma City, by John Michael, born May 8, 1954. All three children inherited their grandfather's gift of song, so it came as no surprise to their parents when the precocious youngsters picked up musical instruments at very early ages. John's considerable musical gifts continued to develop, along with his athletic ability as a baseball player.

Childhood Memories

"I can remember several things from my infant and toddler days," says John Michael, now in his late forties. "There is a picture of me dancing in front of our first television in my birthday suit. I can remember that very clearly, though I was only a baby. I have vivid memories of the high points of the early part of my life. They are all good memories."

What he cannot remember were the uncertain first days of

his life. He was an RH-positive baby with an RH-negative mother, and back in those days many such babies died. Immediately after he was born, he had to have a complete blood transfusion. He says, "To this day I still have an aversion to needles, but perhaps that kept me from using drugs at a later stage!" ⁓ JMT

In the midst of his youthful pursuits, John remembers many inspiring moments with his father. "I have very, very pleasant memories of Dad. I recall the time riding with my father to a sales meeting in a small town north of Indianapolis. On our way back home through the farmlands I was lying on the front seat of our Dodge Dart looking out the windshield at the myriad stars across the rural Indiana sky. I asked him, 'What is God like?' After a thoughtful pause he answered, 'Well son, He is real big.' That simple answer on my childhood level instilled a lasting appreciation for my father's deeper religious thoughts and beliefs. It is amazing how so little can mean so much to a growing child. My dad knew this, and wasn't afraid to share his faith when the time was right."

John continued, "I recall as a six year old having a very special relationship with that big God. One day I was out in the driveway just tossing pebbles into a puddle. I remember clear as day how the Lord created the impression in me that I would either become a doctor or a minister—I wanted to help people to know this goodness that I was then experiencing. But since the sight of blood has always made me sick, I guess that left me with only one option!" John smiled as he related the incident.

Non-Resistance

When I was about ten or so, my parents got me a BB-Gun. I believe that it was a Christmas present. I had previ-

ously been allowed to target shoot a 22-caliber rifle they had given my older brother, so they thought that I was ready.

Blackbirds had besieged us. Therefore, my father told me that it was okay to shoot them. I went to the backyard that opened onto a large field belonging to School 106 in Indianapolis. I targeted a large bird, and shot.

To my surprise it did not fall despite a clear hit, but kept walking away from me. I fired again. Once more the bird kept going. Again I fired, and I could see the BB pound the poor creature. Still it did not fall. Finally, after five or so shots at about three feet out, the bird turned and ran right at me screeching with an agonized death sound. It then fell over dead. I was stunned. These were not merely targets, but living beings with emotions and thoughts. I knew that I had done something for fun that was utterly terrible. I would never forget that feeling of regret. From that day forward I began to think about the terror of taking life.

Much later I came to believe in Christian non-resistance. Of course, there is clear Church teaching that encompasses this, as well as for those who feel that just war is their calling. For me it was tested personally.

On one occasion a friend had gotten quite out of his mind through some kind of drug. He went a bit crazy, and went on a rampage through the farm I was living on at the time. He was overturning heavy lawn furniture and screaming wildly. Something had to be done to stop him before he hurt himself, or someone else. He had picked up a big picnic table bench and was swinging it at those who tried to calm him down. I remember praying that Jesus protect me, and as he swung the bench, I walked right into its path. I fully expected to be hit, and hit hard. But instead of being hit and knocked down, I was unharmed, and was able to put my arms around the guy, and subdue his physical violence.

I recall a similar story from George Fox, the founder of the

Quakers. *He had been teaching on non-resistance, and a man came right up to him and hit him with a heavy beam. He too was unhurt. The attacker repented and converted on the spot. Later, after the meeting the same man asked if he could try again. Fox told him no, for the anointing of the Spirit had been on him during the meeting, but he would be seriously hurt without that special anointing!*

Right after I started wearing the Franciscan habit in public, I had this belief tested in a most peculiar way. I was in Akron, Ohio, playing a Christian coffee house, and was still a bit nervous about the habit. I had just left my hotel room to meet the sponsor in the lobby to get a ride to the concert. I walked past two very big truckers on their way to their rooms, and one made a snide remark. But I did not get angry, and felt that I had been rather victorious over my inner anger. Then, the Lord said, "Go back, and give them a blessing." I felt like saying, "God, don't push a good thing!"

Even so, I went to the room they had entered, knocked on the door. A man the size of a brick wall answered. I said, "Thank you for the insult, and may God bless you." At that point I fully expected to be knocked off of my feet with a jab to the face. Instead, the man looked very humble, and said, "Thank you." I realized that the way of God's peace is under the protection of God if one is really willing to suffer physical pain out of obedience to the Lord. — JMT

The young man inherited more than the treasure of his grandfather's musical talent. He also received a special grace—the deep inner desire to serve God totally and to seek a vocation appropriate for the task. There were, however, a few unforeseen stops along the way for the youthful pilgrim.

Seeds of Faith and the Sounds Unlimited

When John was seven years old, the Talbot family moved from Oklahoma City to Little Rock, Arkansas. This transplant, which was difficult for the entire family, proved even more disturbing to young John, who had come to love their home on Oklahoma City's Wilshire Boulevard, a place he still remembers as an enchanted chapter in his childhood. And just when Little Rock had begun to feel like home, the family was suddenly uprooted again, when Dick was transferred to Indianapolis in January of 1963. Both Jamie and John remembered this particular move as the most stressful of all because, compared to the informality and warmth of the American South, the people of Indiana seemed cold and distant.

The tight family life that the Talbots experienced was not only a reaction to relocating the household to unfamiliar territory. It was also a fortuitous step toward an uncommon nurturing process that helped to foster the talents and personalities of the individual members—particularly in the areas of creative imagination and music. "We found it nearly impossible to make friends in Indianapolis," John's mother remembered. "I have no doubt that this problem contributed greatly to the children's involvement in music—they missed the popularity they had enjoyed in the other two cities." Spurred by their desire to break the local ice, they plunged into the music world under big brother Terry's leadership and found themselves increasingly well known and well received around the neighborhood and at school functions.

The Talbot kids were also well known among their peers for their highly imaginative recreational endeavors. Cowboys, Indians, and the world of childhood make-believe are one thing, but real neighborhood theater, complete with props and custom-designed wardrobes, is quite another altogether. The children of the area, and occasionally their parents, were held spellbound for hours as the three aspiring actors performed well-rehearsed skits and dramas based on popular television shows or widely read children's stories.

A young John Talbot meets the real "Tarzan" (Gordon Scott) – that's John on the left.

Of the three children, John was by far the most keenly expressive of his creative imagination. For him the world of normal youthful make-believe merged with reality—it was occasionally difficult for him to distinguish objective facts from the fiction of theatre.

"I think this was the earliest sign to us of Johnny's deep faith—that he believed so totally," his mother told me. "One day Terry and Tanni built a wall of cardboard boxes around John and told him he was in prison. He actually believed he was hopelessly confined—I arrived in his room to find him crying, paralyzed by his absolute certainty that those boxes were as real and solid as any brick jailhouse wall!" It took some coaxing and more than just a little motherly persuasion to get Johnny out of his prison.

The Talbot family at Christmas, 1959: Dick, Jamie, Terry, Tanni, and John.

John trusted so completely in the myths surrounding Christmas that he refused to accept Santa Claus as merely make-believe. When a classmate ridiculed him for continuing to regard Santa as a real person, his parents decided that perhaps it was time to tell him the truth. At first, John was adamantly opposed to giving up a cherished dream, but eventually he acquiesced with genuine grief. "We had to be careful with Johnny, because while we didn't want people to laugh at him, we also had be sensitive about how we broke the spell of childhood fantasies," Tanni recalls.

When John was not role-playing or toying with his first musical instrument, a drum set, he spent much of his time alone. From the beginning it appears as though John sought out quiet places and natural settings just to sit and think. Nature in itself was a constant source of simple joy to him. He ponders one of those moments, recalling, "I immensely enjoyed trees, creeks, fields, and other living things."

Even as a grade-school youth John's love of nature prompted unsettlingly pointed and mature thoughts, preserved in the painstaking scrawl of a particularly insightful elementary-school essay:

THE FOREST

"The forest is a green carpet of life spread over the layer of death called earth, which all living creatures return to after dying. In it there are creatures of all shapes and forms. There are running rivers of cool, clear water, which bring life into the forest. It can also take life away by the warm, black chemicals of all kinds, which destroy the life in the forest and turn the green into a deep, deadly red. The life in the forest reminds us there is still hope of having a peaceful world. Soon there will be no forest in the world and all there will be is hate and the red layer of death we call earth."

There were times when John's love of solitude, nature, and exploration led to brief episodes of family panic: for example, the young naturalist's spontaneous little outing into the woods near his home at age four. Happening upon a moss-covered "fort" undoubtedly constructed years before by other children, John settled in for a few hours of reflection while his family anxiously combed the neighborhood for signs of the wayward waif. He would never forget his first "hermitage in the woods" experience—a dream that would eventually blossom into fulfillment.

It would be unfair to think of the young John Talbot as an introvert or as socially maladjusted. His natural leanings were simply toward quietness and occasional solitude. In other ways he was a typical youngster. When it came to baseball, for example, he was the all American kid, with mitt, bat, knees torn out of his pants, and more than his share of athletic ability. Baseball was to be the only thing in his growing years that would rival the world of music.

Although he was fond of the quieter things, John was a normal, rough-and-tumble schoolboy.

John recalls, "I can still remember my Uncle Lloyd saying 'Ol' John. I believe that if we opened up his head, little baseballs would fall out!'"

Music, though, was a central feature of the Talbot's family life, one of those avocations around which they wove much of the fabric of their lives. Dick played the violin in the Oklahoma Symphony Orchestra, Jamie could frequently be found at the piano, and the three children would eventually pick up a score

John (second row, third from the left), in 1965 with his Little League team. John often said that if he hadn't gotten involved with music, he would have continued as a catcher.

of instruments, ranging from tambourine to cello.

John remembers beginning piano lessons when he was six, eventually dropping out, but maintaining his musical interests in general. "There was, shall we say, a not quite active but not really passive drive toward music—it was just part of our family life— it was simply *there*," John recalls.

But things began to change when older brother Terry picked up the guitar one day at age eleven. A casual family pastime suddenly became, for the Talbot children, an alluring pursuit full of fun and possibilities.

"It wasn't long before Terry decided he wanted to start a band," John recalls. "He brought some school friends over to the house to play music and sing. I was about seven, I guess, and I just listened, wishing I could be a part of it all. I knew I wanted to sing, and when I actually tried, it felt incredibly rewarding, like I was giving expression for the first time to something deep inside."

But John's enthusiasm was dampened by an unusual problem: he could hear harmonies perfectly but had serious trouble with melodies.

One day after school John came home and sheepishly announced to his mother that his music teacher had flunked him. "What?" she exclaimed incredulously. "You, Johnny? That's impossible!" She marched to the school with her son firmly in tow and politely requested a meeting with the teacher. "I know Johnny can sing," she explained to the music teacher. "He can sing better than any child his age that I've ever heard, in fact. But sometimes, well, he gets a little nervous. And another thing you should know—he only sings harmonies." A second chance for John demonstrated to his teacher that while the youngster faltered slightly in melody parts he was brilliant in picking out and singing harmonies, especially in high ranges. That point was made and John received an A in his music class that semester.

His confidence restored and enthusiasm ignited, John listened intently as Terry and his friends honed their skills singing folk songs in the family living room. When the fledgling group encountered vocal complications, Terry would ask John to arrange the parts in question. This, coupled with his ability to hit what for others were impossibly high notes, gave him an increased sense of belonging to the group. "I could hit a high D or high E with no problem. Most high tenors do well to reach B-flat. And so, Terry began to invite me to participate, in spite of the age difference between us. At nine I was close to being accepted as a member of what we were loosely coming to regard as a band."

The musical instruments that John eventually mastered included guitar, banjo, dobro, pedal steel, bass—the list goes on, but he will always recall with special fondness that first drum. "Dad gave it to me as a gift and of course I played around with it pretty regularly for awhile. Then one day I watched in utter amazement as a guy on TV played a banjo—I was totally captivated. Immediately I ran to my room and began attempting to transform my drumhead into a banjo. Dad gave me a banjo and I eventually took lessons from Steve Lawrence, who had studied under Jerry Waller, who at that time was considered the best banjo player in those parts."

Meanwhile Terry was fully determined to have a successful musical group. A natural leader and highly charismatic individual, Terry recruited three talented friends from the school choir into a musical combination that also included his sister. They called themselves the Quinchords. (John Michael laughs today, and says that this was because there were five members, and, with exception of Terry, they only knew about five chords!) John's big moment came late one afternoon as he and Terry sat in their bedroom talking things over. "John, you know we need a good high tenor in the group. We need a change. Would you like to help us out?"

Skeptical, John responded cautiously, "Sure Terry, you know

I'll continue to help you pick your parts and harmonies."
"I'm not talking *help*, John. I want you *in*. As a full member
of the Quinchords." John's heart skipped a beat but he con-
cealed his joy with a tentative grin. Terry, Tanni, and John were
now full partners in their budding musical enterprise.

Memories of the Quinchords

*I have many wonderful memories from that time in my
life; riding back from an engagement somewhere out in rural
Indiana in the back of my parents' station wagon singing old
gospel songs to pass the time; or singing on large concert stages
with the Hootenannies that rotated from one Indianapolis
High School to another, or the countless Knights of Columbus
and Shriners dinners, all the way to the Coliseum at the Indiana State Fair, where we finally placed 3rd in the Hootenanny
Contest.*

*Once we were going to Ball State University to see the
Chad Mitchell Trio, and had arranged to sing for them before
the show. That night Chad Mitchell was late. He was apparently known for such things. As the concert time approached
and we readied ourselves to go to our seats, one of the group
asked us if we could sing until Chad showed up. Of course, we
accepted, and went out and did the best thirty-minute set we
could muster, receiving a standing ovation. Of course, we were
too young to outshine the famous trio the crowd had come to
hear. They remained one of our models of a great folk group
with great songs, voices, and social consciousness.*

*One other engagement was particularly poignant. We were
singing at a supper club as the after dinner entertainment. The
set went smoothly, and we reached a dramatic high point with
a song called, "The Dying Convict." We reached the point
where the convict is dying, and appears before God when all of
the sudden there is a commotion at a table in the back. To our*

shock a man had a heart attack, and had died right there! It was a sobering moment that caused me to take stock in the themes and lyrics we were singing, even at that early age.

~ JMT

John Michael's first official singing group, The Quinchords, from a promotional photograph in the early 'sixties.
John, the banjo player, was the group's youngest member.
Big brother Terry is third from the left.

"I recall a turning point in my decision about music," John says today. "The Quinchords had been booked to play an outside church festival at Prentice Presbyterian. It was the same church where the Little League met. We were onstage playing, and it went very well. Out in the crowd were team managers, coaches, and players. We were reaching them in a way that was more universal that baseball, 'America's pastime.' I think I knew then what choice I would make."

Inspired by such contemporary folk artists as Peter, Paul, and Mary; the Chad Mitchell Trio, and the New Christy Minstrels, the Quinchords knuckled down to serious practice sessions. John, while finding music fun and expressive, soon discovered that success does not come without hours of hard labor, endless practice, calloused fingers, and late nights. Raw talent itself is simply not enough. By twelve he was relentlessly pushing for perfection.

In September 1967, Terry and John entered their group, now called the Four Score (John says today, "There were four of us, and we knew a few more chords by then!"), in a "battle of the bands" contest at the Indianapolis Young American Fair. They not only won the much-publicized championship but landed a recording contract as well, punching out a crisp little single entitled "Little Brother," which was aired on local radio. Although the influence of the Byrds and the Hollies, two internationally famous groups of the day, is apparent on the cut, a specific and unique style had begun to emerge from the group. It wasn't rock 'n' roll, western, or purely folk, it was an elusive, appealing blend, a distinctive sound that would evolve throughout their career.

Four Score turned out to be a brief transition between the Quinchords and what would become a more successful group, the Sounds Unlimited, which featured John squarely in the middle of an extremely promising combo as rhythm guitarist and vocalist—all at the tender age of twelve.

"That was a real turning point," John recalls. "We became more professional. Terry especially became educated to the possibilities of being a top regional rock 'n' roll band. We began to tour the local area and drew surprisingly large crowds, mostly working weekends at teenage dance clubs, high-school proms, parties, things like that." In the meantime, Tanni was forced to drop out of the band because of illness, but she continued to follow the progress of her brothers with great interest.

In the mid-sixties, John Michael (left), now a young teenager, in a promotional pose with Sounds Unlimited. "Shades of Sgt. Pepper," says John.

John and Terry ate, drank, and slept music, building a brotherly alliance that would blend more than just their complementary voices—they pooled their growing musical talents and business sense into a well-oiled machine that landed the Sounds Unlimited in dozens of newspaper columns, radio shows, and magazine articles. In March 1967, *Teen Tempo* magazine featured the brothers and their band in a five-page photo spread, heaping praise on the young Talbots.

When asked how his overall childhood was affected by youthful showbiz pursuits, John responds philosophically, "I was in a professional environment from the time I was nine or ten years old; of course, there are liabilities. For example, occasional sibling conflicts were often left dangling until after a performance. You know, the show must go on! So in that respect, professional considerations sometimes eclipsed personal needs, but never to the point of a real crisis. On the positive side, I would have to say that it gave us a real sense that there were things much bigger than our own petty problems—ideas worth sacrificing for." He goes on to point out another advantage of life in a band. "I've always said my road experiences, even at age twelve, prepared me for the rigors of life in a Christian community. We had to travel, eat, sleep and perform together and make it work—we learned collaboration and mutual respect in very tight quarters at early ages."

When I realized how much time these kids had invested into their new venture, I had to ask how this affected their schooling—how did they balance the Sounds Unlimited with their school obligations? "Well, needless to say that was quite a challenge," says John, who has an IQ above 150. I was always in the upper level of my class, although I must confess that professionally related absences made things rather tough on us at times. Our parents promised the school authorities that we would be kept current on all subjects, to which the teachers responded with, shall we say, guarded cooperation. I don't think we ever let them down. And our classmates were highly supportive. They saw us as being a part of the newly-emerging youth culture and were fascinated."

The one area where the teachers and the Talbots clashed was, certainly by today's standards, somewhat trivial: hair length. By then, John and Terry wore their hair long enough to cover the top of their ears and brush their collars. In the eyes of the school principal, this was scandalous. "We began to associate long hair with more than stage presence," argues John. "We associated long hair with people who were making statements of social relevance in a very troubled world and we were serious about moving the same direction ourselves. It was a visual image we felt we needed to be identified with. The school authorities fought us every step of the way. When you stop and think about it, both sides wasted a lot of time acting and reacting on this issue, but it was important to us then, of course."

As for spiritual things, John summarized his earliest recollections of church in just two words: "incredibly boring." While he loved thinking about God and was intrigued with this mystical prophet named Jesus, his view of established Christianity tended toward the negative. It just didn't seem to match his intuitive notions of religious ideals. God somehow seemed to speak more clearly, more perceptibly, to him through nature. He saw trees and water, in particular, as symbols of deeply rooted, changeless absolutes in a fast-paced, transitory world, and of the softness of humility and God's love being able to cut through even the hardest rock in time. The leafy branches, and gentle waves of water whispered to him in the breeze; it was God's language.

He did have two profound memories of church that were positive. The first was of pastors who preached with great conviction, yet without theatrics. The second was of his older brother and sister singing harmony during the congregational hymns. Both were related to music. The pastors also happened to have Martin guitars and Gibson banjos, and loved to play almost as much as they loved to preach!

Mason Proffit –
A Brand New Sound

The Sounds Unlimited continued to pull themselves together through more rehearsals, performances, and tedious hours of practice that would frequently sail off into jam sessions, which allowed spontaneity and unbridled musical enthusiasm to burst forth in crescendos of wild sound.

"Hey, guys, we are on to something." Terry leaned over his electric guitar with an unmistakable look of ambition in his eyes. "I think we can make it happen—recording and touring— I mean hittin' the whole damn country, not just local stuff." His voice, hoarse from practice, was calm and deliberate, but the edge of elation at the prospect of hitting the jackpot was definitely present as he spoke. And the elation was catching. The contagion rocketed John to his feet. Record producer Bill Trout seemed the right person to assist the fledgling group into the world of professional entertainment on the national level. After a long meeting, Bill summed up his thinking. "You guys have real potential, there's no doubt about that. Go heavier on the folk, lighter on the rock 'n' roll, and dump the psychedelic stuff. John, you're one of the best banjo pickers in the Midwest, and Terry, you have what it takes as a folk guitarist. Why don't you load up that folk sound with bass and drums and see what comes out?"

"We felt it was important to have a new name for the group," John remembers. "We went home, put our brains to it and came up with a name based on Credence Clearwater Revival's first record, calling ourselves the Mason Proffit Reunion, later shortening it to Mason Proffit. We liked the name Proffit because Frank Proffit wrote the song "Tom Dooley." We chose Mason because it had a kind of gutsy folk feel about it—maybe there was a subconscious tie with mason jars—I don't know."

John and Terry as The Talbot Brothers, before Mason Proffit.

Terry then insisted that a recognizable visual image was necessary to package the group. They looked to other groups

who served as inspiration. The Byrds had become a bit too slick, too polished in appearance, and the Flying Burrito Brothers, well; they had turned to flashy custom-tailored cowboy suits. Ultimately, they settled on an American woodsman look, complete with leathers, buckskins, and hats,

At age 15, and on the road with Mason Proffit.

giving them the appearance of a ragged band of buffalo hunters. They let their beards grow and their hair flowed like General Custer's.

1968 –
One of the
first Mason
Proffit
promotional
pictures, with
Terry seated,
and John
Michael on
the right.

Mason Proffit showed up at events previously scheduled for the Sounds Unlimited. They were an immediate hit with the crowd. Everywhere they went there were invitations to return.

So the Talbot brothers and their growing entourage packed their instruments and buckskins from town to town, captivating audiences who identified with their plaintive cries for equality, justice, and brotherly love. They became tunesmiths, crafting parables and rhymes wrapped in foot-stomping rhythms. John and Terry collaborated on the songwriting. John specialized in the music while Terry's strength was in writing lyrics. They became an unbeatable team. Their creativity seemed to blend as compatibly as their voices.

Terry and Songwriting

> *Terry was the one who taught me how to write songs. He was taking a poetry class in college to hone his lyrical skill, and he shared a lot with me. He had me write a song a day for almost a year. Then he would go through them, tearing them apart line-by-line and note-by-note: "Why did you use that word here, or that chord there?" he would ask. It was devastatingly painful. But it was absolutely necessary, and I owe him for sharing that discipline with me. Without Terry I would not have learned how to be a songwriter.* — JMT

The band, now consisting of five members (John, Terry, Tim Ayres, Art Nash, and Ron Schueter) were playing to packed houses and standing ovations by 1969. They continued to develop their sound with a special emphasis on very tight three-part harmony, unusual for popular musicians of that time. They adapted folk music to rock and social commentary to create what John called "a kind of social comment, folk-country". Then the heavy percussion seemed to give them more of a rock 'n' roll feel. Their eclectic approach made them tantalizingly elusive to those seeking to pin them down with stereotypical adjectives. They were simply Mason Proffit, an exciting new band with a novel sound.

The band's initial invigoration quickly turned into a cool-headed approach to career development. The next move was into the recording studio. They put a record out by releasing what they had intended as a demo tape. Once again, Bill Trout helped. "This is sounding pretty good, boys. Why don't we go with it? Let's sell records to anyone who'll buy them." It seemed like a rather freewheeling approach, but it worked. With the release of their first album, *Two Hangmen*, the Mason Proffit

1968 press photo of Mason Proffit.
Left to right: Terry, John, Tim Ayres, Art Nash, and Ron Scheutter.

band hit the road running. They encountered nothing but wild acclaim everywhere they performed, much to the annoyance of some other bands. "A problem began to develop with the more established bands we toured with," observes John. "We played with the bigger hit acts and trend setters of the era—Iron Butterfly, Arlo Guthrie, Janis Joplin, the Byrds, the Flying Burrito Brothers, the Youngbloods, and Canned Heat. We appeared with the Nitty Gritty Dirt Band, Fleetwood Mac, The Grateful Dead, Jefferson Airplane—I can't remember them all now. I do remember a young blond entertainer who sometimes opened for us, then us for him, when he was still on the college circuit—John Denver. The problem was that we often upstaged the top billing. With us, crowds went berserk. Terry would start preaching as the band vamped, and worked the crowds into a real hysteria. They would scream, clap, yell, and tear up seats when we performed, and then level out when the main act appeared."

In retrospect, with the quickening professional pace and touring schedule, Terry and John now feel that at the time, they had lost their way spiritually. To fill the void, they clung even more tightly to the causes celebrated in their music, pumping out their message with near evangelistic zeal. They were now at the very center of a questioning counterculture—they were among its elite spokesmen. As John says, he had become "a revolutionary, lyrically prophetic, free-living folk-rocker."

Mason Proffit was on a roll, heading for the top, riding the wave of revolutionary fervor that almost tore the nation in two during the troubled late sixties and early seventies. The Talbot brothers, along with the new Byrds, the Flying Burrito Brothers, and Poco, were pioneering a new sound that would later come to be known as "country rock," a sound that would one day make groups like the Eagles enormously rich and famous.

Many of the band's album cuts were radio favorites, and Mason Proffit's fans will immediately recall such hits as "Freedom," "500 Men," "Eugene Pratt," "Buffalo," "Jesse," and the chartbusters, "Two Hangmen" and "A Thousand and Two." It's not unusual in some regions to hear some of these tunes on the air today.

In this world of shifting, relativistic thought, John's inquisitive mind was filled with questions about God, justice, morality, lifestyle and the quest for absolute meaning. He searched for an anchor, a rock, a foundation for life in a heaving sea of change and uncertainty. And in a touring rock band, where personal relationships are frequently temporary and sometimes stormy, John, on an almost subconscious level, looked for some kind of intimacy, a relationship that would provide love and stability.

He looked much older than his seventeen years, with a full beard, a solid build, and eyes that had seen a lot—probably too much. And the company he kept was older—more Terry's age, early twenties. So it came as no surprise when a nineteen-year-old beauty just out of modeling school took a fancy to the young band member. "It was a surprise to me," John says with a faint smile, recalling a handwritten note passed to him through a

John with his father, Dick Talbot, who also acted as booking agent.

mutual friend. "It was a brief message that left no doubt about her intentions, and, I must say, I was quite receptive. I guess that's where our relationship started." That was back in Chicago during road tours. "As I remember now, it was right as I was beginning to do some serious soul-searching that I met Nancy." John later discovered that the note that launched their relationship was written not by Nancy, but by her friend!

Their relationship soon blossomed into a dizzying romance. They seemed perfectly suited, even though Nancy was three years older. She soon began spending a lot of time in the Talbot family home when John was out on the road.

Swept up in the passion of young love and the no-holds-barred atmosphere of an increasingly permissive society, John and Nancy became sexually involved early in their relationship. Making no attempt to cover up, John invited Nancy to live with him in the Mason Proffit "band house" in California. John knew his parents would disapprove. "But what could they do?" he asks. "They were suffering serious illnesses in Indianapolis and we were either in California or on the road. And Terry, God bless him, tried to watch over me in the way older brothers do, but he didn't possess a strong moral perspective at that time regarding my situation."

As things turned out, John had underestimated his father, who demanded that Nancy move out of the house. "You are a minor, John, you know that. And she is an adult." Dick's voice crackled over the phone with uncharacteristic anger. "I'll call in the law if I have to."

In 1971, five months before his eighteenth birthday, John and Nancy were married in an Indianapolis Methodist church. One of John's deepest regrets is the total lack of competent pre-marital counseling he and Nancy received. "Our marital preparation was zip. All we had was our own experience. We went to a pastor one afternoon and we talked about guitars, and that was our counseling."

In the early days of the marriage, John and Nancy experienced the glow and hope of their new start, but it was to be short-lived. John found that his inner search for truth had not ended after all; in fact, following the wedding John felt even more lost, alone, confused. His inner spiritual journey, in spite of its faltering questions and doubts, was becoming extremely intense. He began to withdraw deeper into himself, frequently seeking the consolation of solitude. Less than a month after their wedding, Nancy approached John with sad eyes and more on her mind than she cared to admit—even to herself. "John, we've made a mistake. You should be a monk." He was stunned but not altogether surprised at what had become painfully obvious in recent weeks.

A solemn expression sweeps John's countenance as he relates that pivotal conversation. "Believe it or not, she said I should become a monk. She wasn't a Catholic; I wasn't a Catholic, yet she sensed somehow that I was meant to be a spiritual hermit, a pilgrim moving toward monasticism. I talked her out of it—persuaded her that we could make it work. God knows we tried."

Mason Proffit was on top of the world, winning critical recognition for their recordings and nationwide concert tours. If there were personal adversities being experienced by the boys in the band, they somehow dissolved into the background when the buckskinned idols swaggered on stage to face bright lights and the shrill, charged cheering of their growing number of fans. It was like a powerful drug, numbing the guilt, fear, and pain, and drawing them into a hot rush of exuberant musical abandon. They had become a flagship of this troubled generation, the soul and conscience of a national counterculture movement. At all costs, the show had to go on.

This 1971 press photo was taken at the height of Mason Proffit's success. John Michael (second from right) would soon choose a different path.

The Rocky Road
of Rock 'n' Roll

When one takes a thoughtful look at the pop-music arena, the axiom that immediately comes to mind is, not surprisingly, "What goes up must come down." In the established annals of rock trivia it is possible to find extremely wide-ranging careers, from the likes of Little Eva, whose hit single, "Locomotion," bought her a one-time tidal wave of attention for a few brief months, all the way to the legendary Rolling Stones, who have survived decades of tortuous rock 'n' roll living.

On that scale, Mason Proffit may be found somewhere in the middle, having endured the hungry years of paying their dues while moving toward success, which graced them for about four years. By 1971 they had attracted the eyes and ears of America's most sought-after producers and record companies. Everything about Mason Proffit made them seem ripe for the big time. They were tight and together musically, and ready to face life on the road. They were proven in the recording studio and wrote most of their own material, which was very popular on the concert circuit.

When asked how the band members dealt with one another under the continued stress of demanding road tours, John smiles

A far away dream in the eyes of a young musician.

and relates what seems to typify the occasional stormy moments. "Overall, we got along quite well—we liked each other—but there were times when a disagreement would surface. There would usually be a flash of tempers and a few angry words, followed by business as usual. But there were situations that became rather physical."

John recollects an incident that took place in Racine, Wisconsin. "I'll never forget the time we played one of our first big concerts; four thousand or more people came. Tim and my brother fell into what we thought was a minor altercation during a break between sets. Now, I should explain that Tim had this temper—he was always storming out saying, 'I quit,' but then he would come back later with a cooler head and things would be fine. So as the concert ends, our road manager, Ronnie Sales, is all excited about how well things went and how responsive the crowd was. He was bringing some disc jockeys back to meet us, one of whom was Scotty Brink of WCFL in Chicago, who later became a good friend. By the time we were backstage and Terry and Tim were arguing rather forcefully about something that happened during the show. Ronnie burst into the room and said 'Hi, guys. I want you to meet Scott Brink,' at which point Scotty steps into the dressing room as a bass guitar, thrown at Terry by Tim, flies two inches in front of his smiling face."

John laughs and continues. "Anyone who knows the inner workings of a rock band expects those kinds of things to happen, especially in the midst of demanding tour schedules.

Later there were more profound differences between us, such as artistic direction, but back then things were rolling along in high gear," he adds. "We seemed to attract attention and terrific crowds."

Mason Proffit was a band on the rise. Industry leaders predicted that they would be the next supergroup. Terry, in particular, had an inciting effect on the social protest crowd that inhabited the college circuit of the US. In live performance the band worked a crowd into frenzy that bordered on mania. As the band jammed and vamped Terry would begin to preach a sort of eclectic gospel of social and spiritual consciousness and peaceful protest. The crowds were ripe for this sort of approach, and responded with screams, cheers, and ovations.

"I remember many scenes of working large festival crowds into frenzies," says John Michael. "On one occasion Terry taunted the crowd into unified action saying, "If I were to ask you to shoot out the lights of this place you would do it, right? The crowd responded with wild affirming screams and yells. That night as we walked off the stage, the South Carolina police were waiting for Terry. It took a lot of talking to convince them that it was part of the show, and that no riot was actually intended."

Then there was the drawing power of the personalities themselves—two good-looking, articulate brothers who seemed to charm the masses with their horseplay one minute, and their deeply held social convictions the next. Joe Smith, then president of Warner Brothers, was beginning to feel the excitement of the Mason Proffit magic—they were just about ready, he thought, to step into superstardom. He kept a watchful eye on the group, waiting for the opportune moment to arrive.

Terry was the unquestioned power behind the group. He was the lead singer, and the stage persona of the group. But it also gave him a huge ego at an early point in his life. "I am convinced that if we had become as successful as the industry had hoped for, my older brother would have ended up hopelessly lost, or dead," says John Michael.

Ironically, it was at this very time in the group's professional development that John began to harbor inner questions and doubts about the direction of things, not only relative to the band, but also in regard to his own life. His relationship with Nancy was becoming more unsettling with each new suggestion that perhaps their life directions were more divergent than parallel. In John's words, "Nancy was, and is, a beautiful, wonderful person. She was a good wife and a great homemaker— she was in many ways, what some would call a perfect mate. And I can honestly say that we loved each other." But somehow, young love was just not enough to span the chasm that widened between them and was more ideological and philosophical than physical or emotional. It was difficult to pinpoint the problem. It was simply there, descending like a thickening fog, dampening communication and chilling the atmosphere. Their sheer inability to diagnose specifically the emotional malady they shared created a sense of helplessness and depression—something new for both. But they continued to hang on to hope and to memories of the dream they once held. Perhaps new life could be breathed into the marriage. Maybe there would be a miracle for them.

Beyond his domestic concerns, John attempted to ignore what appeared to be slight inklings of disillusionment with the music industry. "Where is all this going?" he wondered to himself with increasing frequency. "Where does it end?"

He pondered his situation late one evening in early 1971, as the Mason Proffit bus rolled down the freeway toward another concert in yet another city on a heavily booked tour. The muffled howl of the tires churning against the pavement provided the backdrop to John's meandering thoughts. Terry lay draped across two seats, fast asleep, while the drummer, Arty, stared vacantly out the window, rapping his drumsticks against the seat in front of him. Everyone else, exhausted from weeks of travel, slept soundly.

A swirl of critical issues crowded John's mind. Each seemed to demand his total attention but one stood out from the rest: the revolution everyone was singing and demonstrating about. Mason Proffit, in its touring heyday, was taking its band members through the college campuses and streets of America, where a young generation was calling Uncle Sam on the carpet in a big way. Civil rights marches and antiwar rallies were seizing the country in convulsions of national conscience. Even upper-middle-class business executives privately doubted the wisdom of a protracted war halfway around the world that could not be easily explained, even by the Pentagon. As John searched his heart and soul for his role in the protest, he happened upon a very unsettling fact. Those who were shouting down the war in Vietnam were building and detonating bombs of their own. "I saw all this as incredibly inconsistent," John remembers now.

John slumped in his seat, pulled the heavy collar of his sheepskin coat up around his neck, and closed his eyes, wishing for sleep as the vehicle slowed to navigate the streets of the city where they were to play. Peering through the frozen window he fixed his sleepy gaze on a maze of tall stones that stretched out in a uniform network. It was a cemetery.

Death. He was reminded of the growing toll this hard-living business had exacted from some of his contemporaries: Jimi Hendrix, Jim Morrison, and half a dozen other shining lights snuffed out prematurely.

Death

Most religions have a form of meditation on death as an aid to conversion, and fighting worldly lusts. Primitive Observance Benedictines sit by an open grave, prayerfully considering that they may be the next one to die. The Buddhists have an even more graphic meditation on the 10 steps of death and decomposition of a corpse. When besieged with lust, a monk is supposed to meditate on what he now considers beautiful, but as it will appear in 100 years or so. This helps the monk to meditate on that which really brings lasting joy. Through meditating on death we are strengthened in how to live. As I have said, If you are ready to live, you're ready to die, and if you're ready to die, you're ready to live... forever! ⏤ JMT

Being a band on the rise meant that they had access to the established stars of the era. They shared stages, backstages, hotels, and parties with them. John remembers the Eagles, the Byrds, and the Grateful Dead, among many more. On the folk side he recalls John Denver, Arlo Guthrie, and Phil Ochs. They also played with those who would later become country legends, including Waylon Jennings.

And there was Janis Joplin. She was, in the estimation of some, the most exciting female figure in the world of rock 'n' roll. Her raspy, wailing voice and fifth of whiskey had become her trademarks. She appeared hard, but John saw the other side of her one night after a concert, when they shared the billing. He remembered her conversation. It was halting and self-conscious, full of four-letter expletives. They were backstage; the air was blue with cigarette smoke and the pungent smell of pot. Janis took another belt from her nearly empty bottle and joked with the band. But she was really just a lost little girl. John could see it in her darkened, hungry eyes, which searched for approval. She didn't look "long for this world." Still, John and Terry were stunned when word of her death by a drug overdose reached them.

"Janis was like just a regular band member. She hung out with us backstage and talked about regular things. I remember her being disappointed when she found out that we could not stay for her performance. Unfortunately, she sought love from loose sexual encounters that was the talk of the guys of the industry. She simply wanted to find love, but sought it in the wrong way. She ended up among the casualties of Rock 'n' Roll."

Perhaps the tragedies were striking too close to home, for by this time the members of Mason Proffit were themselves experiencing the worldly joys of pharmacological pursuits, along with their roadies and road managers—with the sole exception of John.

"In the early days of the Mason Proffit tours there was some dope-smoking. It wasn't much. Later on, cocaine began to find its way into our recording sessions. If you listen closely, you'll hear the record where it first happens—it was on *Last Night I Had the Strangest Dream*. Despite its pointed antiwar social comment, musically it becomes extremely spacey because the guys were doing a lot of cocaine."

I put the obvious question to him. "What about you? Were you into drugs at this point?"

"No. I never participated."

"Why not?"

"It just seemed that I was having a lot of fun without it — why mess things up?"

"Amazing."

"Yeah. I think somehow God was protecting me—I didn't seem to need the stuff."

"How involved did the others get?"

"Well, one particular evening stands out in my mind. Usually when the guys did dope they were very careful about what they used. On this one occasion they bought what they thought was cocaine, but later it was found the stuff was pretty heavily laced with heroin. Of course, they snorted a bunch of this concoction. I can still remember carrying the guys onto the bus half-paralyzed, unable to walk or talk after our concert. I found it very upsetting."

That cemetery passing by the window said it all. Death seemed to be hanging in the air, riding on the shoulders of pop music's privileged elite. John's thoughts drifted into the past again, this time to memories of a darkened, smoke-filled club in Chicago where he watched Phil Ochs and Arlo Guthrie shoot pool. Everyone was drunk. Talking about his late father, the great Woody Guthrie, Arlo's eyes were wet with tears. Phil was later to commit suicide.

"We played with the Byrds, legendary for their integration of Folk and Country styles with Rock, on many occasions. I remember them playing bumper tag with us on the way to a party in Champaign, Illinois. When we got there they found out that we were driving our own van, not a rental van, and were very apologetic. Later that night I remember Roger McGuinn sitting at a kitchen table lamenting not being able to raise a normal family because of his rock 'n' roll lifestyle. He also had, and still has, a stunning memory of the old folk music repertoire. He was one of my heroes."

These stories represent many, many more that fill John Michael's memories of the stars of that period. One thing was certain: Despite having access to everything they wanted, they remained, for the most part, unhappy. They had access to all the fame, money, sex, and drugs that they could imagine; yet they remained unfulfilled.

John also recalls another repeating experience from those days. "After concerts I would look out over the empty arena floors at a sight that had become too familiar: The floors would be covered with drug paraphernalia, empty liquor bottles and beer cans, and an occasional passed out fan." He began to see this as the fruit of his music, and asked himself, "Is this what you want to stand for?" The answer was a clear and conclusive "no." A transformation was taking root in John's heart.

It was these repeated experiences at the impressionable

young age of 15 and 16 that got John started on the search for spirituality. " In those days we rode in primitive conversions of a regular Trailways bus. They would take out every other row of seats, put some equipment in that space so we could stretch our legs out, and wrap up in blankets to sleep," he recalls. The nice motor coaches standard to today's entertainers and politicians were not on the market yet. Travel was long, and arduous. On those long bus rides across America the band members could sleep, do drugs, or read. John chose to read.

He began to read everything he could find about religion and spirituality. He read about the major world religions such as Hinduism, Buddhism, Taoism, and those from the more Judean heritage such as Judaism, Islam, and Bahai. He read about the religions of the Native Americans he admired so much.

He also read from the Revised Standard Version of the Bible his grandmother had given him in anticipation of his never realized Methodist confirmation as a young man. In all of his reading, the words of Jesus seemed to have a more profound effect on him than any others. He chalked it up to Christianity being the religion of his own culture. But he kept reading. He especially liked Matthew's Gospel, and the Sermon on the Mount. He also liked the Book of James because it emphasized a very practical faith that manifested itself in radical lifestyle, not just in words.

During this time of searching John also prayed. "Every night I would spend time in prayer and meditation. I would ask, 'Who are you God; are you a He, a She, or an It?' I didn't care what the answer was. I just wanted to know." He wanted the experience he was reading about in all of the great religions of the world to become his own. "For over a year I prayed for God to become personal to me."

John's thoughts went back to the club in Chicago with Arlo Guthrie and Phil Ochs. Without breaking his rambling chain of thought, he reached down and retrieved the dog-eared

Bible from his tattered leather bag. There might be some comfort in its pages. He opened the book to a heavily underlined passage and began to read, the circular beam from the overhead reading light illuminating the pages in front of him: "For what is a man profited if he gains the whole world, and loses himself?" These words of Christ echoed in his troubled soul, the question burned in his mind, demanding an answer. The bus rolled on into the damp, chilly night.

John continued to read widely within the field of religion. He began to understand humanity's quest for meaning and significance in diverse cultural settings. He related very well, for example, to the mystical and meditative qualities found in Eastern religions, recalling from his childhood moments of solitude and the sounds of God within. But he also found the nature-filled stories of the Native American religion satisfying in a more earthy sense. "We had special feelings about the Native Americans anyway," John adds. "They epitomized the cry for justice in our music. We thought, 'Hey, these are the first real Americans—the Native American people—and look what we've done to them.' I admired them for their culture, their beliefs, and their legends. It became a real cause for me and, of course, for the band."

John sensed impending revelation. He could feel it about to happen—something special, something to conclusively reward his diligent search. He could never have guessed how overpowering it would prove to be.

It happened in 1971 in a hotel somewhere in mid-America. "Things now rush together in my memory about those years, probably because the endless touring and performing lulled me into a stupefied indifference about where I was or when I was there, and, of course, there were far more important matters on my mind at the time," John points out. "All I remember about the general circumstances is that we were in the middle of a tour, probably somewhere in the Midwest, and spending this particular night at a Holiday Inn. I had my own room—the walls I recall as being blue—probably matched my disposition at the time."

The other band members and road crew were checking into their rooms down the hall as John closed the door and collapsed on the double bed, turning his tired gaze toward the window. The soft eerie glow of the neon hotel sign filtered softly through the drawn blue drapery, bathing him in a pattern of light and shadows. As had become his custom when there were quiet, restful moments at hand, John began to pray to a God he did not know deeply but had come to believe in. Almost imperceptibly, his silent, interior mediation became an audible, vocal question: "Lord, who are you?"

Then it happened. Light seemed to fill the room, gradually intensifying to a mind-bending brilliance. Startled, John sat up, blinking his eyes to behold the figure of a man in white robes, arms outstretched, with long hair and a beard. "I saw an image," John says, "That looked like Jesus—it was a traditional Christ figure—an incredible sight." A surge of adrenaline tore through his body like a hot rushing current, yet there was no fear or panic.

"I looked up out of my prayer and saw Christ bathed in light before me," says John Michael. "He didn't say anything. He didn't give me a "great commission" or anything like that. He was simply present. His love poured over and through me—it even seemed to emanate from me. In that experience I knew that my prayer for God to reveal himself to me was answered in the person of Jesus. I didn't understand any Christian theology. I just knew that God loved me through this revelation of Jesus, and that any of my past sins or failings were forgiven. He stood before me, somehow almost *around and within* me, in infinite greatness yet total humility. I felt compassion. And I felt acceptance. I had been reading *about* Jesus and feeling him in my heart, but at that moment I actually *experienced his touch*. I knew it was

Jesus. From that point on, I begin calling myself a Christian again."

Some would say that this experience was merely a psychological manifestation of his own longing in the image of the faith he grew up with. John Michael admits, "It could have been psychological. But God created me with a psychology, so if God wanted to use it to reach me, then so be it."

As they say, "the real test is in the fruit," and the fruits of John's life were definite changes for the better. John's band mates said that he became a more mature and well-balanced person. His newfound faith was making him a better human being. His was nicer to be around. The photos of Mason Proffit show the change. The early ones show a dull-eyed, aimless teenager. After the Christ experience John Michael looks like a young man with a vision about the direction of his life.

Beyond this primary vision, several more followed over the years. This journal entry speaks of five. ⏤ JMT

Journal Entry from March–April 1978—The Vision

The first vision came one night during prayer, and it was as if Jesus were painting a beautiful picture of a Christian community right before my eyes. It was the most harmonious painting I have ever beheld, for it was filled with love and peace. Selfless love and unity characterized every aspect of this community of Jesus' followers, both in their dealing with one another and with nature. In this vision all of creation was reconciled to the way of Jesus; his followers not only spoke of his way, they also lived it.

The second vision, again given during prayer, called me to an apostolate of poverty among the churches of Jesus. I saw myself clothed in a brown, coarse garment resembling a habit and walking on foot from church to church to share the simple love of Jesus. The message of the apostolate was not the important call of this vision, but rather the mode of the apostolate was. In this vision Jesus called me to a ministry that did not depend on anything other than two legs and a voice to bring his message to the world. Being free from huge expenses, this apostolate could thus be offered to the world as a gift of grace, just as Jesus offered his apostolate to the world as a gift of grace. Only poverty brings the freedom. Only poverty brings the freedom to bring the wealth of Jesus without charge.

In the third revelation Jesus assured me through scripture that although I would lose my home, my wife, my child, and my property, he would grant me the wealth of the kingdom, the family of the saints, and the home of my spiritual mansion if I would undertake this apostolate of faith and poverty to share his love with the world. To this day I still seek to accomplish this in a better way. It is the core of the gospel message, and to it I can only respond, "So be it."

The fourth vision came at a time when I was seeking a unified Christian church for a new spiritual home. I sought and found a church that could ensure the way of the cross and the way of unity based on the love of Jesus through that which he had ordained. In this vision Jesus called me to enter into the Roman Catholic Church, a church I once attacked verbally. He simply said. "This is my ordained church. She has been sick near death, but I am raising her to new life through my Spirit."

The fifth perception came at a time when I was considering the similarity between my call to an agrarian prayer community and an active apostolate of poverty within certain of the religious orders already existing in the church of Jesus. I saw a striking similarity of spirit and action between the visions of St. Francis of Assisi, St. John of the Cross, St. Benedict, and Thomas a Kempis and my own vocational call from Jesus. Granted, many of these orders no longer resemble the visions of the men whose names they bear, but most continue at least in charity, which is the greatest gift, and some are still faithful to their original visions.

⟜ From *Changes* by John Michael Talbot

John does not consider himself to be a "visionary," but he did have other visions back in the first days of his conversion that have guided his whole life. In addition to the vision of Christ, on another night he saw a community in perfect harmony with God, each other and all of creation. He calls this simply, "The Painting," because if he was a visual artist, he could actually paint what he saw. He also was given a vision of an old tattered monks robe, that he later learned was called a "habit' being held out to him by another monk. Among others, he also saw himself walking on foot from place to place, wearing a tattered and rough habit, with a group of people with him. He was told that if he simply stayed in music, God would open the doors for these things to unfold.

"I experienced a positive change in my life. I felt deep love for others, forgiveness, tenderness, new levels of compassion, as if

I had somehow absorbed these qualities from my vision of Christ. I rediscovered something from my childhood faith. I felt that it completed me as a human being. I became a better brother, in the broad sense of the word, to my friends and to the band," he says.

John was never the same after that evening at the Holiday Inn. Like Mary after the Annunciation, John pondered these things in his heart, speaking to no one about the vision for some time. He nourished the budding new life within by even more exhaustive Bible study and deeper times of meditative prayer. But love is hard to hide, and before long those around him felt its warmth.

By 1972, Mason Proffit had reached its peak. All the energy of the record industry, the media, the public, and the developing skill of the musicians themselves had come together into that rare combination, and the band was poised for big-time success. It appeared as though there was no stopping the upward thrust of this team of individuals who, judging from outward appearances, had it all together. But just as the band looked its strongest and big-time success seemed just around the corner, the beginning of the end was at hand.

There is no doubt that the rough lifestyle, including increasing drug abuse by some members of the group, contributed to discipline problems. And there was the general malaise experienced after having to be "up" for weeks at a time during tortuous itineraries around the country—a tiring, abrasive routine that could rub tempers raw. However, the most significant challenges to the group's survival were artistic concerns, according to John. "Our management wanted a marketable, more commercial sound that they thought would sell more records and pump up the demand for appearances. Of course, their interests were financial, not social or artistic. I felt that we should move more toward artistic expressions of folk, bluegrass, and ethnic forms of music in order to more creatively integrate ourselves into the rock idiom. Our management, on the other hand, was pushing us more toward basic mainstream rock, and we resisted that."

This was not a new managerial cry. As early as the first recording, the Talbot brothers were encouraged to use studio players, and some songs written by professional songwriters. Out of loyalty to the guys in the band who they had known for years the brothers declined. John says today, "This decision was one that most likely kept us from attaining superstardom."

It was with a growing doubt about the professional direction of Mason Proffit that John returned home to Nancy, and their farmhouse in Munster, Indiana after a string of concerts on the West Coast. It was February 1972. With question marks about the band looming in his mind, he had turned to prayer and to his deepening spiritual journey for consolation. And it seemed more important now than ever that things on the domestic front should work out.

There was a lump in his throat as he turned his key in the back door lock, braced against the bone-chilling wind and rain. He stepped into the dimly lit mudroom; a rush of warm air welcoming him as he quietly closed the door behind him. "Mustn't wake Nancy up," he thought. But before he could shed his heavy wet coat, she appeared from the back bedroom squinting into the entryway light.

"John. Hi, what time is it? I guess I feel asleep."

"It's a little after two. How ya doin'?" They embraced, standing silently together for a long moment.

"How were the concerts?"

"Oh, they were okay—well, not really. I mean, it feels like we're just going through the motions. The guys don't have their hearts in the music anymore, not like they used to. Terry and I talked for a long time after the last performance and he's feeling the same way. We discussed the idea of working together, the two of us, if things don't pan out with Mason Proffit. We could just be the Talbot Brothers, or something." Nancy could see that he wasn't happy. There was a heaviness in his voice that she had rarely heard.

"Maybe things will come together for Mason Proffit, John. Every band has its downers," she reassured him with little confidence in her voice. "Besides, you have the Ozark Mountain Folk Fair and the other festivals to look forward to on tour this spring."

He winced at the thought. They were booked so far ahead—the tunnel looked so long. The weight of it seemed unbearable.

"Nancy, you need to know—I want out of the band. I want to write and play my folk songs. I can't stand it any more. I wouldn't be truly honest with myself, or with the other band members, if I tried to stay on for the sake of the show."

If there was one thing Nancy had come to respect about her husband, it was his resolute, uncompromising desire to be, as he had just said, honest with himself and others. Sometimes it even frightened her a little because she did not often share John's deeply held convictions. She knew that someday, and maybe in the not so distant future, it would become a serious matter of conflict between them. In the end, she knew that John would have to be, as he said, true to himself, and totally honest with her.

But for now they shared a warm, comforting embrace—a few silent moments together. Only the sound of a cold, winter wind could be heard raking across the roof in a low, mournful howl.

As spring approached, warm breezes coaxed blossoms from the plum and dogwood trees; the sweet scent of the slowly greening forests filled the air in the Ozark Mountains of Arkansas some 500 miles away. The sounds of saws and axes could be heard echoing through the crisp morning chill of

Eureka Springs, as preparations were underway for the first Ozark Mountain Folk Fair, the brainchild of local entrepreneur Edd Jeffords. His director of operations, Bill O'Neill, was working feverishly with his crew to clear an amphitheatre area in the woods at Oak Hill Ecopark, ten miles north of town on Highway 23. In keeping with Jeffords's ecological ideals, many trees were left standing while the rest were used to build the stage and the arts-and-crafts booths around the perimeter of the grounds.

Eddy and his wife, Linda, and a handful of friends, including the Rolling Stones' stage manager, Ted Jones, had worked for more than a year to put together a colossal music-and-arts fair, scheduled for Memorial Day weekend, 1973. It was to be the first in a series. Top-rated bands and artists were slated to participate. Sharing top billing with Mason Proffit were such greats as the Nitty Gritty Dirt Band, the Earl Scruggs Revue, John Hartford and the Ozark Mountain Daredevils. Also booked were John D. Loudermilk, Johnny Shines, Kenneth Threadgill and the Velvet Cowpasture, Zydeco King, Leo Kottke, John Lee Hooker, the James Cotton Blues Band, and "Big Mama" Thornton. It would be a wild and free celebration. Local merchants were not enthusiastic, but consoled themselves with hopes of hearing the uninterrupted ringing of cash registers.

"I can honestly say that this was during the time of the peak of our career," John states confidently. "In spite of our problems, we pulled ourselves together for that touring season, and the festivals. It felt like the old days once again. We were more than ready."

"There was a vague sense of finality going into that particular festival. All the bands we respected were there," John remembers. It was as if the whole band knew that this would be their last big performance together, but the subject was never broached as they flew over Missouri and into northern Arkansas. They talked about the scenic rolling mountains and

51

the beautiful countryside.

"Over the previous year or so the band had seriously investigated buying land outside Tucson, Arizona, or Golden, Colorado. But it didn't feel right to a bunch of Midwestern boys. This felt more like home. So we said, 'Let's buy some land— if we use it, fine, and if we don't fine.' We knew it would be a safe investment in any case. Once we pulled into Eureka Springs, we knew this was the place. We checked into the Crescent

1973 – John Michael's last tour with Mason Proffit.

Hotel, where most of the other acts were also registered, and settled in for the weekend," John recalls. "It was so nice out, I went out on the hotel lawn for a breath of fresh air, and just lingered out there for a long time, drinking in the view which overlooked Saint Elizabeth of Hungary Catholic Church. By the way, Saint Elizabeth of Hungary was the patroness of the Third Order of Saint Francis, which I didn't know at the time, of course. Ironically, I did not know that Saint Elizabeth's was a Catholic church either. I now find this a highly symbolic incident in my life, pointing toward something I could never have dreamed at the time."

"I remember it was early evening and I was so relaxed, looking out over the landscape, that church, with its statue of Jesus and the Sacred Heart. I closed my eyes and breathed a prayer and I felt the Lord say very distinctly within my innermost heart, 'Buy land here.' The very next day we contacted a realtor, Clell McClung, whom I later learned was one of the most active parishioners in Saint Elizabeth's, and we scoped out the area. Then and there, Terry and I bought a couple pieces of land. It was a beautiful wooded valley, nestled between high, rolling hills. It felt strangely like home to me—it was a kind of déjà vu sensation. I knew it was right."

It was half-past seven on Friday evening, May 25. The sun was setting behind the Ozarks and the folk fair was officially underway. Thousands of vehicles converged on little Eureka Springs—campers, trucks, vans, dozens of bikers with their wild-looking Harley choppers and a whole lot more out-of-state license plates than the locals had ever seen at one time. Architect–professor Robert Austin was the master of ceremonies and rolled out the red carpet to one band after another. The jubilantly receptive crowd had grown to well over ten thousand and appeared to one local-newspaper reporter like "a swaying sea of blue denim." Paul Johnson of the *Arkansas Gazette* called the event "a multi-sensory experience."

The boisterous throng eventually swelled to more than thirty thousand. Almost every type of intoxicant and narcotic could be found in the place; cocaine, grass, alcohol, and more were eagerly and openly consumed. "The huge natural amphitheater seemed from some distance away like a suddenly awakened volcano," reported Johnson, referring to the marijuana fog that settled over the valley. Young vendors hawked water-melon and corn on the cob and it seemed that cases of beer were stacked by the ton near all the concession stands.

Steve Vanhook of the Times–Echo newspaper in Eureka Springs noted that the Earl Scruggs Revue was a highlight, judging by the crowd's applause for the "King of Banjo." The Dirt Band was also a hit, teaming up with Hartford and Scruggs for a show-stopping jam session. The most generous comments by critics, however, were reserved for Mason Proffit. In the words of one reporter, "The hit act was Mason Proffit, a foot-stomping, bluegrass-rock band that had the crowd shouting back responses to shouted questions. The act ended with the lead singer advising the crowd not to lose the good feeling that was evident on the hillside. 'When some guy starts beating you on the head,' he advised the crowd, 'just give him a big wide grin; it drives them crazy!'" Apparently, Terry still couldn't resist a short sermon between numbers.

When John and Terry leaned into their microphones with banjo, pedal steels and guitar and began to sing the ballad, "Two Hangmen," the crowd burst into unrestrained applause, then just as quickly hushed themselves to listen, some singing along quietly. "Eugene Pratt," an anti-Vietnam war comment, stirred up the masses as its melody drifted out through the valley. When John finished the beautiful ballad, "Sail Away," he brought the throng to their feet. The band closed their set only to be shouted back to the stage.

John Michael at the 1973 Ozark Mountain Folk Festival near Eureka Springs, Arkansas.

While sharing a motor home dressing room with the Scruggs Revue, John rehearsed one of his "breakdowns" with Mason Proffit's fiddler, Bill Cunningham. After they got it right

Earl came over and said, "That's real good, John." "Coming from Earl, that was like Moses speaking to the chosen people," he says today. John felt pride for the quality of the band. They had become quite good after years on the road.

John remembers surveying the crowd, seeing them as lost flock of sheep looking for a leader, searching for an answer. "There was an awful lot of dope, free lovemaking, nudity, drunkenness—I felt a deep caring and compassion for them. Even as I played and sang, even as I felt that old stage rush of adrenaline, I was at the same time stricken with a kind of grief." He learned a little about how Jesus felt when a crowd of thousands looked to him for sustenance, and he fed them all with one boy's lunch of bread and fish. "Let me be obedient and giving, like that boy in the Gospel story," John whispered prayerfully as he scanned the more than thirty thousand festival participants. "Let me somehow feed people with the truth, with the bread of life."

1973 – Ozark Mountain Folk Fair – Mason Proffit's crowd tended to 'let it all hang out', and enjoy the good-time sounds. Alone on a hillside as the festival continued, John felt the Lord leading him to buy land in the area.

For many of the musicians, the event was kind of nostalgic reunion. The Mason Proffit guys had hung out with the Nitty Gritty Dirt Band in Aspen, they knew the Scruggs people from Nashville, and had encountered most of the others from their years of travel around the country. So it seemed only natural as the folk fair drew to a close that they should all gather on stage on the final evening for a grand finale of folk and bluegrass standards, capped with a last song, "Will the Circle Be Unbroken?"

John Michael remembers the jam sessions on the porch outside of the gathering room on the top floor of Eureka Springs' Crescent Hotel. "Leo Kotke, John Hartford, the Dirt Band... we all had a blast jamming with musicians we respected and liked."

For John, it was to be a special event, marking, in a way, the end of an era for him, leaving bittersweet memories of the Mason Proffit band at its all-time best.

Back at the hotel, which has a commanding view of the surrounding mountains, John loaded his gear and prepared to depart for Indiana. He paused, inhaling the fresh mountain air laden with the fragrances that heralded the onset of summer in the Arkansas forests. He turned toward the horizon to look in the direction of the beautiful property he now owned, and was greeted by another image—the figure dominating the Eureka Springs skyline that had become one of the area's main tourist attractions: an immense statue with outstretched arms, a beard, and long hair. It was the Christ of the Ozarks.

Breaking Up

The 1973 Ozark Mountain Folk Fair is still remembered in Eureka Springs; in fact, the place will probably never be the same because of it," John muses, fingering the tattered newspaper clippings that have yellowed over the years. "That event led to other festivals and concerts, and, I think brought some folks permanently into the Eureka Springs area who would otherwise have never come."

The land he had purchased would serve from time to time as a pleasant reminder that he had a piece of "paradise" awaiting him in the future—maybe someday he would return, he thought, and build a ranch or small farm. He could grow his own food, write music, and raise a family in the woods of the Ozarks. This was an image he would cherish for years, and would call upon it for consolation in the months following the folk fair, as the life of the itinerant rock band began to dissolve like a dream at dawn's first light.

Perhaps it was more of a nightmare than a dream. After months of agonizing about the band and his own journey in life, John pulled the plug on Mason Proffit and, along with his brother, quit the band.

When John and Terry left the group, Mason Proffit became history, even before their Warner Brothers recording contract

1973 –
Still under contract
with Warner Brothers
for one more album,
but now without a band,
The Talbot Brothers
released their first
Christian album,
an award-winning
record called *Reborn*.

had expired. One album remained to be produced, so John and Terry put their heads together and came up with a plan. "Here we were with an album to record and no Mason Proffit," recalls John. "So Terry and I cut an album. We used some of the best players you could get into the studios. Finally we got together with Warner Brothers and handed them this record saying, 'Oh, by the way, this is a Talbot Brothers album, not Mason Proffit.'"

After the Talbot Brothers released their first Warner Brothers album, they took to the road to perform in a string of folk clubs and college campus concerts. In Atlanta they noticed that Roger McGuinn of the Byrds was playing the same club a week before them. They had gotten in a few days early, so Terry decided to check out his show. John Michael stayed at the hotel and continued an intense time of prayer and study that typified that period of his spiritual journey.

John says, "Terry had a chance to talk to Roger at the club. Terry shared his newfound Christian faith. When Terry shared about the Holy Spirit, Roger had an interesting response. He said, "Yeah, it's kind of like the space between the molecules when you're tripping." Roger had "kind of" gotten the point! But he may have understood more than John or Terry thought. Years later he would give his life to Christ.

The same held true for many well-known, and not so well known secular artists in years to come. Some found a solid spiritual path for their lives, others burned out from the rock lifestyle. For the most extreme cases this often meant a tragic death. It typified that the choice really is one of life or death, and the death can often be both spiritual and physical.

John and Terry hit the road to promote the album but understandably received very little support from Warner Brothers. John asserts, "It was an excellent album, called *The Talbot Brothers: Reborn.* We used Randy Scruggs, an accomplished young flat picker, Josh Graves on dobro, and David Lindley from Jackson Browne's band on lap slide, Russ Kunkel on drums, and Leeland Sklar on bass, both from James Taylor's band. It was a beautiful album—we did our best vocals ever as a duo on that record. And another thing—Terry had become a Christian during that time. It was right during that time that Terry became very serious about his commitment to Christ."

Terry's journey was similar to John's in that he rationally thought through his questions and searched for answers in various religious traditions. Terry glows as he relates his transformation.

One of the consequences of the Talbot brothers' conversion to faith in Christ was a sudden proliferation of songs that testify to their changed lives and philosophies. Their first album as a duo for Warner Brothers bears a distinctly Christian mark, particularly in the cut "Hear You Callin'":

I hear you callin' me,
I hear you callin',
In the weepin' of the willow tree
At dawn.

Jesus, how I believe in you,
Can't keep from cryin' when I think
Of all the pain you knew,
For so long.

And you know I will always stand beside you,
You know I will always keep Your light
Growin' in my mind.

Oh, I hear you callin' me,
I hear you callin',
In the weepin' of the willow tree
At dawn.[1]

Although the energy of personal conversion is clearly transmitted through this album, their social concern still breaks through. In another cut, "Trail of Tears," John laments the fate of the Native Americans, hearkening back "to Wounded Knee to count the dead." Throughout his career John has maintained the remarkable ability to empathize with oppressed people through his music.

"Then something terrible happened," John jokes today. "I met other Christians!" It was no longer enough to simply love Jesus and try to follow His way of life. "Now I was being told that if I didn't understand a particular fundamentalist theology, and learn how to quote scripture for the occasions of my life, and especially those of my sinful band mates, I couldn't really be saved." John had met the Jesus Freaks.

"I found myself heading toward a crisis point," he says. "There I was, this young Christian, I wasn't trained theologically, I wasn't locked into a single church, yet I was desperately hungry for more of God. I was looking for true spiritual authority to which I could submit myself." He began reading with a vengeance—the Bible, Bible commentaries, and books by Francis Schaeffer, Dietrich Bonhoeffer, Hal Lindsey, and a host of others who also had a strong fundamentalist bent.

"I was reading, consuming, grasping. I was beginning to lose that simple, open love. I was living in a subtle kind of fear; a fear that said 'You don't know all you need to know.' I was made to feel that I had to memorize a lot of Scripture before I could be truly accepted by my Christian brothers and sisters. It was a smothering sort of spiritual self-consciousness."

Over the next months, John surrounded himself with a wall of books that became for him a virtual prison, as real as his childhood jailhouse trauma. He had been exposed to fundamentalist Christianity, which, in its dogmatic certainty and zeal, represented a kind of false harbor of security. He had a clear, rigid set of rules to live by and doctrinal explanations that provided a sense of stability and definition for a world that was unstructured and full of change.

"I began to push the Bible too legalistically. Slowly, but very surely, I became a walking, talking Jesus freak who had a quote from Scripture for every conceivable problem. If you had a problem, I had a verse. I had become the proverbial 'bible thumper.' I entered into what I call a caricature of Christianity rather than a full, beautiful painting of Jesus, which would be vibrant with color, subtle shadow, power, and gentleness. At this stage of things I believed as I was taught: that this particular brand of Christianity, narrow as it was, represented the only real truth. Everyone else was just a little off, except Catholics, who were way off."

"The Jesus Freaks began showing up at my concerts, and at

airports. They all had an excitement about their faith that I liked, but they also had an adamancy and anger that was not good. Unfortunately, I could not tell the difference at the time."

He was argumentative, and his prodigious reading had provided him with an impressive vocabulary and an array of theological weapons for every occasion. He could leave some poor soul sputtering and stammering with a wounded spirit and damaged faith. In more debates than he cares to remember he would convert his opponent to his own fundamentalist position. "I talked many Catholics out of their Church—it was frightening. I convinced them that they couldn't be saved in the Catholic Church with all that idol worship and repeated ritual. Sometimes I even scared me!"

Nancy, too, became disturbed. She wondered to herself, "Who is this person I'm living with?" Obviously, she had trouble relating to John because she had not subjected herself to the same rigorous study. She just knew something was wrong, and was getting worse. And she didn't like it.

"If someone had an issue, I had a bible verse," he recalls. "Even if they didn't want to hear it, I made sure that they did. Within a couple of years I became a terrible person to be around. What's worse is that I did all of this in the name of the very experience that had so changed my life for the better through genuine love. I began to lose my friends, my band mates, and soon I even lost my family."

Initially, Nancy had followed John into a relationship with Christ that became her own genuine experience. The catch came, however, when she realized that the path she was following as she sincerely attempted to live out her Christianity differed drastically from John's more intense approach. The common faith that should have bought them closer together was, ironically, driving them even farther apart. At the same time, just as Mason Proffit had broken up, the Talbot Brothers duo had also vanished into thin air.

"It was a rugged time," John admits. "I wasn't really working, just painting houses to bring in some money. I grew a two acre organic garden and would go around the neighborhood with sacks full of green beans to sell to neighbors for a few extra dollars—a big change for a guy who only a couple years earlier was singing to twenty thousand people and earning real good money. And that had to be difficult for Nancy to deal with. After all, she married a successful rock 'n' roll star, and all of a sudden she's confronted with this seeking, searching, almost flipping-out poor Christian man. Big change. But I have to say, she hung in there with me when most women would have called it quits."

With a faltering marriage, lack of work, and an increasingly confused approach to his Christian faith, John found himself in a spiritual desert. His own conscience even turned against him: Can I play rock music and still be a Christian? Should I even play music at all? And what about ecology? Should I drive a car, pollute the environment, deplete petroleum reserves, and contribute to an evil system based on greed and power? And what about diet? Shouldn't we as Christians eat only natural foods, and only certain ones, like vegetables and grains? He was seized by subtle, but very real fits of scrupulosity. Indeed, self-condemnation seemed to stalk him at every turn. He sunk into a maze of ethical and philosophical questions from which he could not break loose. He had become a prisoner in his own mind. Maybe, he thought, maybe I'm going crazy.

Or perhaps it was the test to which he was put in order to explore the darker regions of his own being—the classic desert experience that seems to befall so many true believers who seek the kingdom of God. The serious pilgrim must slay his dragons, cast out his demons, and fell his giants. For that indefinable "dark night of the soul," as Saint John of the Cross called it, will either take your life or purge it like a refiner's fire in the private, lonely crucible of interior crisis. "It is especially when it is making progress," Saint John writes, "that the soul encounters darkness and ignorance."

To Saint John of the Cross, a sixteenth-century Spanish mystic, people of true spiritual greatness were more often distinguished by darkness than by luminous, spiritual assurance. (It is interesting to note that Saint John went on to build monastic communities that were dedicated to prayer and to a stark, simple lifestyle, a way of living to which John Michael would later be drawn.) Saint John of the Cross championed the cause of contemplative prayer when he said, "Let those who are great actives, who think to gird the world with outward works and preaching, take note here that they would bring far more profit to the church and be far more pleasing to God if they spent only half as much time abiding with God in prayer...assuredly, they would accomplish more with one piece of work than they do now with a thousand...to act otherwise is to hammer vigorously and accomplish little more than nothing, at times nothing at all; indeed, it may even do harm." [2]

Eventually John would read those words and ponder their deep wisdom. He would also study the writings of Thomas Merton, a Trappist monk who echoed for the modern world Saint John's call to contemplation: "We will communicate only the contagion of our own obsessions, our aggressiveness, our egocentric ambitions, our delusions about ends and means, our doctrinaire prejudices and ideas. We have more powers at our disposal today than we ever had, yet we are more alienated and estranged from the inner ground of meaning and love than we have ever been."[3]

Merton's answer for our problem is meditation and contemplative prayer. This was the tool with which the troubled young musician would use to pull himself toward reality, toward sanity, toward faith. In the midst of his shaken world, John began silently and regularly to pray deep, simple prayers. It was as though he were starting over, with his vision of Christ still occupying the central position of his anxious thoughts.

In the spring of 1974, John's strength began to grow. It was early May and he was out alone for a walk on a particularly beautiful Sunday morning. He and Nancy had decided not to go to church—he had rationalized to himself that nature and the outdoors are just as much a sanctuary as any church building. He stopped, peering down at his heavy hiking boots, then visually tracing the moss-filled cracks that marbled the concrete of the old sidewalk. He felt good about himself for the first time in ages—he seemed to have a grip on things. Somehow, the unresolved questions didn't seem so pressing. John breathed in the cool fresh air full of springtime and marveled at how the months had flown since the previous May, when Mason Proffit dazzled the multitudes at the Ozark Mountain Folk Fair. Now those days were gone forever; the dream had died as natural a death as the rock world is capable of dishing out. He smiled to himself as he laid it to rest once again in his mind.

And it seemed like just last week, or even yesterday morning that he had trudged into the house from his beloved garden with huge globs of dirt on his boots. Taking them off, he shuffled toward the kitchen sink to wash his hands when Nancy fluttered in, bags of groceries awkwardly balanced in each arm.

"Did you make your doctor's appointment? He asked absentmindedly.

"I was late, but I made it in."

"Well?"

"Well, I'm pregnant!" Nancy squealed in unrestrained delight, awaiting her stunned husband's response.

"All right!" he shouted, embracing his wife, dumping over a sack of groceries, and knocking her off balance.

"We reacted like the kids we were," John chuckles. "We were very happy with the news. There was a kind of unspoken expectation between us that this would cement our relationship for good—it would bond us together and save the marriage."

"We were so happy," Nancy recalls. "We celebrated right there in the kitchen. But deep down inside I think I also felt fear—John wasn't really working and I wondered how we would support a growing family." Their elation temporarily overshadowed the practical concerns that would weigh upon them.

A few hours past midnight on May 9, 1974, Amy Noel Talbot was born after an 18-hour labor. John and Nancy had just finished cleaning up after his late-night birthday party. Twenty years old, and now a father—would he measure up? He thought so at the time. But he would have to do better than he did in the delivery room, where he very nearly passed out.

He would find work. Just maybe he and Terry would get lucky with their music again. They had been collaborating off and on over the past few months, playing and writing songs. They had hopes of reviving the Talbot Brothers team. But it wasn't happening. Perhaps they'd get things going in the summer. "Don't hold your breath," Nancy playfully warned, only half-joking.

"Nancy was looking for a comfortable Christian life, you know, nice clothes, nice car—standard family life. Although I was mellowing at the time, having discovered meditation and prayer, I was still asking myself, how do I live out my Christian beliefs? My beliefs were based on my perception of a Gospel that demanded simplicity, sacrifice, and total commitment. So when I would talk about living on a farm, Nancy probably pictured a larger, modern, automated farm, while I was thinking about a secluded little log cabin in the woods. Our ideas were just different," John explains. "My ideas were much more radical and much more simple. Hers were much more normal—I'll readily admit that. It's not that she was seeking luxury. She just wanted an average American lifestyle—I can't fault her for that."

"To me it seemed that John was straying from reality. I tried to be supportive, to be a good loving wife. And I think I was. John was constantly reading and writing—activities in which I was not involved. We weren't touching each other's lives anymore because he was lost in a world of spiritual things that I could not grab hold of."

John remembers discovering the crux of their crisis—that they hadn't truly understood the very idea of marriage in the first place, and this was further complicated by their extremely divergent concepts of Christianity. He shuddered at the idea of divorce or separation, although that sometimes seemed the only logical conclusion. We have to make it work, he determined.

As in many pressured marriages, finances played a significant role. John, much to Nancy's chagrin, didn't seem to care at all about money. It even seemed to be his enemy, or at least an unnecessary complication, while she regarded it as a tool, a certain measure of security for the family and the future. One would think that record royalties, residuals, and concert receipts would have provided a hefty monetary cushion, and for a while it did. As is so often the case with successful young bands, however, funds began to disappear.

"In plain English," John recounts, "we were ripped off. We were unexpectedly caught in this tax bind and when we looked into things, far too late, we found we had been taken advantage of. Those we had trusted took us for a very expensive ride. Terry and I learned some hard lessons," says John, looking back with forgiveness on the culprits.

But forgiveness doesn't pay the bills, and John began to realize he had to round up some cash. So there he sat one day at home, feet propped up on the kitchen table, rocking back in a groaning wooden chair, looking like a logger from the Yukon with his heavy, faded flannel shirt, aging Levis and well-worn, thrice-repaired high-topped boots. The phone rang, jangling the silence and very nearly upsetting the balancing act. Scrambling to the phone, John buried the receiver in his shoulder-length locks.

"John, Terry. I've got a proposition for you, little brother."

"Let's hear it."

"Well, you know we're putting Mason Proffit back together—"

"Yeah, Terry, but you know I can't really…"

"Wait a minute, will ya? Listen to me, now. I want you to open for us, okay? We are all singing for Jesus anyway. What do you say?"

"I say, when do we start, brother?"

"The Talbot brothers ride again! I'll call with details."

"All right. I'll get back to you."

Back on the road—and bring on the banjo, he thought with glee. And the paycheck. The time is right. John bounced into the bedroom. Nancy was feeding Amy and wondering why he was staring at her with that gleeful grin. John shared his plans. "You and the baby could come along," he insisted. She responded with guarded optimism.

Jesus Music

My first encounters with Jesus Music were through my sister, who had fallen in with the E Group, an early version of what would later become Petra, and some kind of house or loose community that they were a part of in Indianapolis. She was dating a guy named Randy Mathews at the time, who had produced a recording through a Gospel Music outfit out of Waco Texas called Word Records. He was quite impressed with Mason Proffit because of our Christian leanings. His record seemed an interesting attempt to combine Gospel and Contemporary styles. Only later would we discover that Randy was one of the real pioneers in Contemporary Christian Music.

Some years later, after the break up of the original, and regrouping of the now Christian version of Mason Proffit, did

I meet Larry Norman. He had befriended my brother Terry in California. The Christian regroup had come together at Valley Presbyterian Church, and its coffee house called Jonah's Place. I met Larry during our booking in Vail Colorado in conjunction with a secular club we were playing.

Larry was truly good to us. He took promo pictures of the band, and generally hung out with us, while teaching us some of the ropes of the newly emerging Christian Contemporary Music world. During that time we also met Richie Furray from Buffalo Springfield, also the founder of Poco, and the Souther, Hillman, and Furray Band. It was great meeting a guy who was a bit of a legend, but it was even greater because he was quite serious about becoming a minister. He later became ordained in the Maranatha churches, originating out of the California "Jesus Movement" phenomenon.

It was from this form of Mason Proffit that I would meet another big influence on my life, Billy Ray Hearn, who would become a lifelong friend. ⁓ JMT

"It was about mid-1975 when Terry put the band together and back on the road," John says. "It was just small-time touring. They weren't what Mason Proffit had been, but they were good and played a circuit of bars, pubs, and auditoriums, drawing as many as three thousand or as few as a hundred. I began to open for them and I found that when I pulled out my dobro and my banjo, people loved it. I even began getting standing ovations before the band came on."

It was John's reentry into music, and it felt good. He was given the opportunity he had always wanted—to test himself as a solo performer. The response was exhilarating. It was also a chance to perform with Terry once again.

The new Mason Proffit had attempted to swing a deal with Arista Records that eventually fell through. John looked elsewhere in the recording industry. It was then that he met Billy Ray Hearn, an executive with Myrrh Records, a well-known Christian record label.

"I met Billy Ray at a Christian music festival in Colorado Springs. He was there to conduct the orchestra for Nancy Honeytree, one of the best well-known female artists at the time. He was also driving the van from the hotel to the concert site. In one of those rides he played an album by a group called the 2nd Chapter of Acts. It was stunning. I had heard much of the new contemporary music, and, frankly, until then I wasn't impressed. They were the first group to sound good on record. Later, after our closing set, Billy Ray approached me about the new Mason Proffit making a recording for him. I told him that I was leaving the band, and that this was my last concert with them. He offered me a record deal on the spot. I sent in my demo as soon as I returned home." It was made on an old jam box over an old cassette tape, but the raw energy of those first songs was undeniable.

Billy Ray Hearn

Billy Ray was my main mentor in Christian music. If I came to find a whole new family of brothers and sisters in other musicians and writers, Billy Ray would certainly qualify as my father figure regarding Christian music, just as Father Martin would later become my spiritual father in the Church and St. Francis. Billy Ray took me in almost sight unseen from our first meeting in Colorado Springs at that first Jesus Music Festival. He would produce many recordings for me, and would give me great encouragement and support. Even though we did not always agree, I always respected and seriously listened to his input regarding my music ministry.

Later, when I became a Catholic and recorded The Lord's Supper, The Painter, *and* Come to the Quiet, *the Lord spoke very clearly and said, "Billy Ray is the man but Sparrow is not the company." We reflected that in releasing all of my recordings on the worship branch of Sparrow, Birdwing. After Birdwing was discontinued, we began to experience increasing tension in the company relationship. It would be Billy Ray and Phil Perkins who would help give me the courage to start Troubadour For The Lord, and find a way to reach Catholics more effectively without alienating the CCM crowd too much.*

—JMT

Billy Ray, an easygoing man with smiling eyes and a soft, engaging Georgia-turned-Texas accent, seemed the perfect person to talk to about the Christian recording business, a relatively new phenomenon generally dubbed "Contemporary Christian Music." John found it to be a world unto itself, with a growing constituency, its own record charts, even its own periodicals, award ceremonies, and rising stars, such as Barry McGuire, Larry Norman, Pat Boone, Jamie Owens, John Fisher, and scores of groups. Many of these entities had emerged from the Jesus movement and were now perfecting their music within their own self-contained business world.

A number of the artists were Christian celebrities, that is, entertainers with established reputations who had moved from secular to Christian music but who generally had been regarded as stars before their involvement with Christian recording. Others could be called celebrity Christians, personalities emerging from within the Christian community and not widely known outside of the Christian music market or the church-performance circuit. John could perhaps be best seen as being among the Christian celebrities.

What John could not have known then was that Billy Ray was busily working behind the scenes to start his own record company in a bold business move that would eventually be highly successful. Sparrow Records was soon launched.

An enduring business partnership and a meaningful friendship were born. John began to record, using mostly his own material, and once more hit the road, touring the West Coast and the Midwest. Sparrow Records would soon become a great success.

1976 – John Michael begins his career as a solo Christian artist.

"I was finally a solo performer, doing what I really wanted, which was writing my own music, recording my own albums, and doing it all for the Lord. I was all His. And it helped the domestic situation in a limited financial way. But I would have to say that it hurt the marriage, because I was away a lot on tour. On the occasions that Nancy did come along, I would frequently play little coffee houses and prayer groups where the people were a little threatening to her in their sometimes extreme ideas. But I felt it was good—it was, in a sense, a new beginning," John concedes.

To many of those radical Christians, John was quite literally a godsend. He was an honest breath of fresh air in an increasingly commercial religious environment. His lyrics were prophetic and challenging, but the music was mellow, smooth, even haunting. Talbot cut a rugged image with his worn jeans, work shirts and long—very long hair. "I wanted to be about ministry, not entertainment," John points out. "I found that there was still a lot of Mason Proffit in my musical style, and

John appears at an
outdoor festival at the
Jesus Barn outside of
Peoria, Illinois in 1976.
That year, he would
release his first solo album,
John Michael Talbot.

although it was technically
correct, it wasn't suited to
my new goals. I attempted
to drive home the message
with both social and spiritual content but was relying
on technical performance rather than the guiding of the Spirit.
I would prepare people for a good time with an up-tempo
piece, follow with a subduing series of songs, and then drop the
hammer of conviction with an serious, emotional selection."

While John sensed a satisfying emotional response, he was
somehow left with a feeling of spiritual emptiness. The message
was not moving most people on a deeper level. His concerts at
times felt like hollow victories, although sales of his first Sparrow record, *John Michael Talbot,* were encouraging. Then one day,
John sat down with Barry McGuire, a Christian musician best
known for his secular hit "Eve of Destruction" and his role in
the Broadway musical *Hair.*

"Barry, your music touches people—it reaches people. I've
seen it and I want that ability to minister," John said. Barry sat
silently, stroking his beard, squinting thoughtfully skyward.

"Well, brother, *you* don't reach people. You sing to God. You
worship God and talk to God while you're onstage, and let *God*
reach the people. He can do it better than you can."

Barry's simple yet profound words of advice penetrated to

the depths of John's heart. "Barry McGuire is very much responsible for a tremendous breakthrough in my music ministry," John affirms. "I began to encounter other artists who were living by that rule—Nancy Honeytree, Phil Keaggy, and others. Sometimes they would sing, play, and say the same things at every concert, yet people were moved deeply because it was God touching those lives."

A subsequent realization began to gnaw at John—the problem of church affiliation. By the time his second record, *New Earth*, was released, John was grappling with this issue, just another in a chain of challenges confronting him as he grew and matured in his craft and in his Christianity.

"I was becoming more popular—I had begun to worship God in my appearances, which, as a consequence, became very, very good. I was doing eighty performances a year and couldn't keep up with demand," John observes. He had become an established member of the Christian music scene by 1977. He was emerging as a leader and a spokesman.

"The thing that amazed me about other Christian artists, many of whom were becoming my friends, was that they were all rooted in a church, balanced in their ministry, and grounded in humility. In contrast, I was a loner, not submitted to ecclesiastical authority, and highly confident of my abilities, my interpretation of Scripture and my prophetic role. I began to want authority, I wanted to "be humble," and to submit to an elder or teacher—it was a real process of maturation for me. I continued to seek. Later I would learn that humility only comes from experience, and if you ever think that you have it, you have surely lost it."

Things may have been developing well in John's ministry and music, but all was not well at home. Once the thrill and novelty of parenthood and of new recording contracts had worn off, he was once again confronted with realities of a failing marriage. It was a heavy emotional burden but not one he was willing to freely share. Marriage problems were not supposed to be found among minister–musicians. After all, they were teaching and preaching to hungry crowds about how to live.

"I began to keep up a nice Christian front, you know, that I'm the together young leader. I know my Bible, I'm charismatic, and the gifts of the Spirit are working in my life. Isn't my family wonderful? Isn't my ministry successful? These ideas were like prerequisites for a public ministry. The whole time, my ministry wasn't what I wanted it to be, nor was my family life. Once again in the commotion of my life, I was in trouble. Serious trouble," John admits, referring largely to his marriage.

There was a sudden rash of divorces among leading personalities in the evangelical Christian world—especially in the music-ministry crowd. This was a terribly shocking development, not only for this network of friends, but also for their growing constituencies. "I just couldn't let it happen to me," John says. "Divorce was viewed as a real scandal; I think it still is. Maybe in some ways it should be. But forgiveness was sure hard to find, even among the friends of those unfortunate enough to endure this tragedy. While divorce represents real failure and sin, and while we know that God hates divorce, we are not called to condemn people. We are called to love."

In the midst of emotionally stormy times, of nagging self-doubt and setbacks, John held tightly to something that no one could ever take away—the vision, the reality of spiritual rebirth, the commitment to the loving Christ he had encountered. This was his rock, his anchor of reality, even when Christian pursuits themselves became troubling, and at times, even oppressive.

In John's mind, his Christian witness to the world and his well-received music ministry were on the edge of ruin. How could he continue to be a real Christian or an inspiration to others if he could not even work out his own marital problems? What if divorce is inevitable? What will the media say, what will Billy Ray think, and our parents? The questions multiplied in his troubled mind. He was determined to turn the tide.

With this goal in mind, he bought every book he could find on marriage and family counseling. "I began to bring home these books on sexuality, psychology, parenting—everything I could find. We read them together. We even considered joining Francis Schaeffer's community in Europe. We knew there had to be an answer—it was just a matter of finding it. Though things were tough, I knew we could work it out," John says, remembering his feelings during those difficult days. "I would go out on the road with this awful feeling deep inside, and be away from Nancy and Amy and desperately want to get home. Once I was home things were so fragmented and tense that I would find myself wishing for the road. I needed an answer. I needed resolution.

"I remember doing a concert very close to home, and asking Nancy to drive over with the baby and stay the night in the hotel. At first she said yes, then later decided to only come for an hour or so in the afternoon. She also brought a girlfriend who was encouraging separation and divorce. As she drove out of the hotel parking lot I think I knew deep inside that she was leaving the marriage as well."

It came sooner than he could have dreamed. "I think it would be best if we simply separated as friends," Nancy announced one day. "I want a separation. I can't handle this anymore." The words were spoken softly, but they struck like bullets.

Today John remembers sitting with Nancy on the stoop of one of the farm outbuildings, talking about things for a

John, Nancy, and daughter Amy in 1976, shortly before the break-up of their marriage.

couple of hours. Afterward he would go on long walks, crying tears of confusion, and crying out to God. She began to socialize with old friends, and stay out late at night. Both were in a state of confusion and sorrow.

John had imagined in his worst nightmares that this was an option she might choose, but the preparation did not blunt the shock he felt through his whole being. And he knew she meant it. There would be no turning back, judging from the force of her words.

Nancy recalls those moments vividly. "I was supportive for as long as I could be. When John was going through his fundamentalist phase, I stood behind him. But after a while I lost it, and I was the one who needed support, but John couldn't provide that for me, and I understand that. Things that I couldn't buy into were matters of deep conviction for him."

Broken and heartsick, John went to live with his parents in Indianapolis. The separation ultimately led to divorce and proved to be, without a doubt, the most painful time of John's life. Over and over he would ask, "How could this be happening to me?" The events merged together in his mind, churning like a storm-tossed sea, flooding him with a sense of impending doom.

"I've attempted to boil it all down in recent years and I have come to some basic conclusions," John observes. "Nancy was called to be married to an ordinary Christian man, the kind who works eight hours a day, Monday through Friday. On the other hand, I was called to be an artist, a contemplative, in some ways a poor hermit. As a musician on the road, my life was erratic and somewhat unpredictable. While Nancy was meant to be a good middle-American housewife, I felt strongly called to a more radical lifestyle."

Nancy later remarried. She and John would see one another on occasion and engage in phone conversations, usually regarding Amy. "There has been real healing between us," John assures.

"I consider Nancy and her husband friends."

John sees the pain of divorce as a form of penance. It is a constant reminder of the seriousness of marriage, and in this sense, at least, a kind of mercy. But at the time of his separation from Nancy, John could find no mercy. "I went through absolute brokenness. I was face down in the dirt, confronted with my own failure. It was like death. I found myself identifying in a small way the agony of Jesus. My only comfort was to relate my sufferings to Christ in some way," he says.

"Nowadays I see a double lesson through the divorce," says John Michael today. "Trying to keep a marriage together that is not established in God can be almost impossible. But, if you choose divorce, you can never know at the time the full negative ramifications it will have on your whole family from then on." These are sobering words.

Deeply aware of his own sin and failure, John nevertheless continued to cling to the treasure of his salvation—the vision of Christ still alive in his memory. It was his only consolation—his inner island of calm in the midst of the hurricane that rampaged through his soul. But there seemed to be no promise of a fresh beginning, no energy left to start all over again. The public ministry would have to go—maybe even the music. He would lay it all down at the feet of the crucified Christ before wandering into the desert to seek the path on which he was to walk. He would, he thought, simply withdraw to his own corner of the universe, praying that somehow God would find him useful in some small way.

He had read about Amish communities and Catholic monasteries from his trips to the local public library and the Christian bookstore. John had vague thoughts of going on a trip to visit some of them, beginning in his home state of Indiana. He made it as far as the Alverna Franciscan Center in his old hometown of Indianapolis.

It was there that he met Father Martin.

Tracking the Path
of St. Francis

He had worked at his craft for a decade, since the age of ten. Calloused fingers and many hundreds of handwritten pages of songs testified to years of diligent practice and creativity. He had managed to survive four taxing years of life on the road with Mason Proffit and had become a spokesman for a generation of young people seeking truth and justice. Having weathered many storms, he seemed to have emerged on top of things with few real scars. John Talbot's resilient spirit and raw determination had always seen him through. That is until his world, including an extremely promising future as a Christian musician, had been turned upside down.

In the spring of 1977, feeling like a condemned man, he offered the house and nearly everything else to his wife, seeking temporary solace in the warmth of his parents' home. It was a harbor of safety, a kind of halfway house as he entered one of the most severe transitions that a man can face. Already, he missed seeing little Amy. Two years later, John wrote these words in his journal:

I see my daughter, and my heart yearns to be a normal father for her. She loves me deeply, but because of Nancy's remarriage, the reality of my being a normal day-to-day father is impossible. I see her confusion and her questions, and I cannot answer them. I am moved to great sorrow. Soon her presence stirs a great love and great pain within us both, so that I am nearly unable to be around her and still keep my composure. I am truly sorry that this little girl must suffer from the mistakes of my youth, yet no matter how sorry I am, it seems that both she and I must suffer this separation that neither of us really wants. This is my lifelong penance I suppose, for whenever I see this little child I am unable to hold back the tears that well up within my penitent soul.

John and Amy play during a visit to his parents' home in 1978.

The dissolution of John's family produced a sorrow that was compounded by the uncertainty of his professional future, not to mention his frightening doubts about his spiritual journey. He needed help—he needed counsel. For someone who has enjoyed esteem in the eyes of others for so long, this can be a very difficult admission; however, a broken spirit and a contrite heart had borne the fruit of humility in John's life. He observes that the full dimensions of his conversion to Christ were released only when he plunged into the fathomless depths of contrition created by the sense of failure he felt from his divorce.

"When I was on the road with the band, I looked around and saw that the people around me weren't happy—they didn't possess the real keys to life. And I began to deduce from my readings that there was something more to this existence, and that perhaps the peace I sought was spiritual. I was working my way into what I now recognize as the beginnings of a conversion. I would call that a conversion of attrition. It was only after the failure of my marriage that I was blessed with a further conversion of contrition, a contrite spirit based in a kind of godly grief—a painful yet wonderful grief," he says with irony. He was down, with nowhere else to look but straight up. He felt overwhelmed by the realization that he had broken God's heart. It was through his remorse that true conversion was perfected and completed. The gift of repentance was now his.

John was drawn to Alverna, a Franciscan retreat center only two miles from his parents' home in Indianapolis. He knew of a priest there who was reputed to be an expert marriage counselor. After reading *The Journey and the Dream*, by Murray Bodo on the life of Saint Francis of Assisi, John thought a Franciscan might be able to answer a lot of his questions—even if he was a Roman Catholic.

"I had been reading about Saint Francis—about his incredible devotion to Christ and his stark, simple life that has always appealed to me. I could relate to the power of his conversion. And my other readings—books on the early church, the writings of Bernard of Clairvaux, Thomas á Kempis, Theresa of Avila, John of the Cross, and Thomas Merton—were all ministering so deeply to my spirit, yet, I was troubled because they were all Catholic! I needed some understanding, and I thought that this Franciscan priest, Father Martin Wolter, could provide it," John remembers.

But his inquiry was not without its disappointing moments. Following directions to the Alverna compound, John drove his van down the long, narrow driveway, his heart pounding in anticipation. He envisioned a modest wooden structure with habited priests prayerfully walking the grounds with heads bowed. What he actually saw as he wheeled into an expansive parking lot was something quite different.

"When I drove into the complex I was appalled. Looming up in front of me was a castle—a huge stone castle circled by neatly manicured lawns and shrubs. I knocked on the door and an African American woman answered. I thought, oh, no, these guys have servants as well as a mansion! I later learned she was on staff, and paid well. I asked for Father Martin. Another Franciscan brother came to the door in street clothes and said that he didn't know where Father Martin was. I told him I was interested in asking questions about Catholicism and Saint Francis. He informed me that he couldn't be bothered now because he was fixing the air conditioning. I left very angry, as I'm sure you can imagine. What I saw was a far cry from the brown habits and modest living I read about," John explained.

But John felt God calling him back to the Franciscan center. "As I was speeding out of the place, God spoke to my heart saying, 'haven't you ever had a busy day when you didn't want to talk to people?' The answer was affirmative. So I went back. It was then that I met Fr. Martin for the first time. I found him to be a wonderful Franciscan priest. He was in his mid-sixties but very young at heart, and extremely wise. In talking with him I found a man who understood the spirit of renewal, tradition, and how practically to live the Franciscan life in a modern world. He is a very loving, kind man, and has been my spiritual director ever since."

Not only did John strike up a warm and stimulating relationship with Father Martin, but he came to know and love the others friars at Alverna, who were to become part of a new support system for him as he worked through the challenges that seemed so hopelessly overwhelming at the time.

"Tell me about yourself, John," Father Martin asked with inviting, smiling eyes that twinkled in the subdued light of his library.

"Well, I hardly know where to begin, Father." As a fundamentalist it felt odd to call someone other than your Dad, "father." A lump filled the young man's throat, as the emotional load of his current circumstances seemed to learn upon him with increased weight. He felt just a little awkward—almost as if he were at a kind of confession—but the prospect of unburdening his heart before a willing soul tipped the scales in favor of full, detailed disclosure.

"How about just beginning at the beginning," Father Martin offered.

John shared the history of his musical career, his vision, his conversion to faith in Christ, and finally the tragedy of his divorce. Numerous times he fought back the tears, but bravely and frankly he told his story to the only person he had met who seemed able to draw it all out of him in one sitting.

Father Martin

Fr. Martin Wolter, OFM, is my spiritual father in the Church. He has also helped immensely with the founding of the community. If I am the spiritual father of the Brothers and Sisters of Charity, then he is the grandfather.

Fr. Martin has been an instrument of God on countless occasions. But he is also quite human. He loves to talk. His brother Friars call this "one hour Martinizing," after the old

> laundry slogan. They also say, "Martin doesn't think that God is speaking unless he is talking!" There are many humorous stories one could tell on Martin, and the friars do not hesitate to do so, with obvious love for their brother Friar and priest.
>
> My experience is that the Word of God is there in a human spiritual director for those who have the patience and humility to wait. God speaks his perfect word to us through human vessels. On many occasions Fr. Martin has just "shown up" or called at the right moment with just the right word to encourage or challenge me. Nobody told him. He was just praying and God inspired him to talk to me. He has done this many times with all the people who love him so much.
>
> I like to call this the "Yoda syndrome," like the little spiritual master in Star Wars. If we can learn to be humble and patient under spiritual direction through imperfect elders, then we can gain the nugget of the Word that is within this human package. Fr. Martin can make me a little crazy at times, but he has without question been the instrument of the very Word of God for me in many more times of crises and trial. I owe him my entire spiritual life in Christ, the Church, and community.
>
> ～ JMT

"John, I want you to think and pray about coming here to stay for a while," Father Martin ventured after several hours of intense conversation. "You need some space, some time to think, and a supportive environment, and you could study in the areas that interest you, such as Catholicism, community, and Franciscan spirituality."

Without a moment's hesitation John responded in the affirmative and plans were immediately made for him to lodge at Alverna. The first matter of business they would handle together involved the divorce. Then they would talk about vocation, which meant dealing with John's profession as a performing musician. This would be supplemented with a study of Roman Catholicism and church history. And of course, they would look into the life of Saint Francis of Assisi.

John rushed to his parents' home to pack his things, about a ten-minute job in view of the fact that he simply didn't own much anymore. It seemed he was forever giving things away. As he loaded his van, he recalled a curious dream he had had some months earlier that hadn't made a lot of sense to him. In this dream a mysterious unseen force drew him toward a castle in the woods. Once he was within its shadow, men cloaked in brown robes came out and surrounded him, handing him a similar garment and inviting him to stay. "We will teach you how to live," he heard the robed figures say.

As he recalled the dream in more detail, his excitement grew until he could scarcely stand it any longer. It had been from God, he concluded. It was a fantastic confirmation that he was walking on precisely the right path. He had never experienced such a sensation of deep comfort and high adventure simultaneously.

Once situated in his new surroundings, John felt very much a part of the Alverna family. He remembers feeling as though caring people were nursing him back to health. He thought of it as a kind of womb-like environment, where he lived in a temporary cloister waiting to be reborn-again.

He would spend long hours in prayer, Bible study, and reading, occasionally breaking for long refreshing walks through the nearby woods, down by a churning creek that meandered through the property. He listened to the wind rushing through the trees and took delight in feeding the squirrels and chipmunks. The place was special, almost enchanted. It is alive, he thought, with the spirit of Saint Francis, and somehow blessed by the Spirit of God in a unique way. There was the inexplicable feeling of home about the grounds and buildings, a sense of family among its inhabitants.

June 1978

> *Jesus is the example we use for obedience. He submitted to the will of Father in the authority of men. Jesus always condemned hypocrisy in those in authority, but in the end he submitted unto them as unto his Father, even at the cost of losing his life, but it was in this that he was raised to eternal life. In death he found life. If we obey those in authority, we too will come to lead others in Jesus.*
>
> ⁓ From *Changes* by John Michael Talbot

Father Martin soon set about the business of mending John's damaged ego and shattered emotions by working through the issues of the divorce in a direct but compassionate approach. "I had heard about how unyielding and judgmental the Catholic hierarchy could be on the issue of marriage and divorce, which made me a bit apprehensive. But Father Martin was so amazingly empathetic—it was as if he had endured the same thing. He had the ability to feel what I was feeling. Yet, along with his tenderness, he pointed out my shortcomings and moral responsibilities in no uncertain terms," John states. "He helped to rebuild me from the ground up. Or maybe I should say, from my heart out. It was a welcome time of healing on a very deep level for me."

Then late one night, early in the summer of 1978, John retired to his small, sparsely furnished room after an evening spent reading about the life of Saint Francis. In one corner were his thin mattress and a blanket, and in another corner an old table served as a desk. Books littered the bare hardwood floor and his guitar rested against the windowsill. He lit a single candle, reclined on his bedding with his well-worn Bible in hand, and prayed, as Saint Francis might have, to find some guidance from the Scriptures to resolve his situation. The following day John made this entry in his journal:

> My wife decided to divorce me, so I was faced
> with a whole new life. I didn't know whether to
> resist her desire for divorce or to look ahead to a life
> on my own. I opened the scriptures three times,
> after the manner of Saint Francis, believing that
> Jesus would honor my seeking his will in faith.
> I opened first to I Corinthians 7:17, which says,
> "Are you bound to a wife? Then do not seek your
> freedom. Are you free of a wife? If so, do not go in
> search of one."
> I opened next to Matthew 19:29, which says,
> "Moreover, everyone who has given up home,
> brothers or sisters, father or mother, wife or children
> or property for my sake will receive many times as
> much and inherit everlasting life."
> I opened a third time to Matthew 10:8–10,
> which says, "The gift you have received give as a
> gift. Provide yourselves with neither gold nor silver
> nor copper in your belts; no traveling bag, no
> change of shirt, no sandals, no walking staff. The
> workman, after all, is worthy of his keep."
> While I did not seek separation or divorce, my
> wife asked for both. In keeping with the message of
> these Scripture passages, I did not resist or judge
> her. All I can say is, "So be it."

It was as though the weight of the world had been lifted
from him. Once and for all he could lay this issue to rest intellectually, while admitting to himself that he would bear the
emotional scars of his terminated marriage for the rest of his
life. It would be a penance he would readily assume.

As he prayerfully and thoughtfully considered his marital

situation, John was forced to examine the *idea* of marriage in new depth—its social, emotional, physical, and sacramental dimensions. Out of his meditative prayer on the subject, he exploded with a new awareness of the mystical union between Jesus and the believer. "I began to see the *process,* the *development* of life in Christ. In the West we are so goal-oriented. We want it all *now.* But gestation and birth are a laborious process involving a sequence, a continuum. I began to compare marriage to this idea of union with the Messiah."

He went on to explain in more depth. "In the premarital romantic relationship we learn objective facts about our partner: color of eyes and hair, height, weight, dress, speech, and other superficial, obvious information. Then we abstract our learning phase toward that person's thoughts, their outward looks on life, philosophy, political beliefs, morality, and so on. Once we have acquired this basic data, largely through discussion, we move toward a deeper communication—a physical interaction concluding with sexual union, where the partners merge into oneness. We lose ourselves in one another. We blend. We marry.

"When I applied this concept to my relationship with Christ, I suddenly understood the sacramental nature of marriage and the possibilities for deepening my Christian journey. I began to move toward a more existential, more mystical experience in Christ once I had gained basic, objective information. I realized that the possibilities for spiritual growth were absolutely unlimited! And all this grew out of thoughts surrounding my divorce," John says in amazement. "At first I was enamored with Christian ideas in the early phase of collecting information about Jesus through study and reading. Later, I sought to know the person of Jesus in a love relationship that grows to this day through the communication of contemplative prayer. It was from this painful experience that he wrote *The Lover and the Beloved,* a book that has brought comfort to many thousands of listeners.

The Lover and the Beloved / Mike Leach

Years later, after the initial success of the biography Troubadour For The Lord, *and John's published journals in* Changes, *Mike Leach of Crossroad/Continuum encouraged John to write something on his own. After serious thought and prayer, John agreed.*

As a theme, John used the relationship between a husband and wife to describe the spiritual life according to Franciscan principles. He got this from the famous work of Raymond Lull, a 13th century Third Order Franciscan who lived in a hermitage for nine years before launching an ambitious project to evangelize the Moslems through dialogue rather than by force. John also studied the works of St. Bonaventure, St. Peter of Alcantara, Boniface Maes, and the Carmelite Spanish mystics.

It was Mike Leach who helped him put it together as a readable manuscript. As John's first editor, Mike was much like a first love concerning writing. Mike gently, but firmly, deleted about one third of John's manuscript. This taught John the art of writing to a popular audience. "Mike always reminded me to make my points clearly, and without too many words," John muses. "The experience taught me to share my heart as well as my mind, and to go for the heart when writing for the general religious reader. Mike has remained my most admired writing mentor to this day."

Indeed, many have called the resulting work, The Lover and the Beloved *John's best devotional book. And with good reason. For John, prayer is a personal love relationship with Jesus Christ. In the book, John seeks to help foster this special experience in others by describing mystical life with Christ in terms of the intimate relationship between a man and a woman, or* The Lover and the Beloved.

"And I think it's important to carry the marriage analogy even farther. The natural outgrowth of marriage is children. This is true also on a spiritual level, as we are able to draw more people to Christian faith as a consequence of our union with Jesus. This is the mystical love relationship between Christ and his Church."

Today John still teaches what he learned through his meditating on marriage, and is often sought out for counsel. Ironically, the lessons learned from his own divorce have kept many other marriages intact and vital.

"What about my music, Father Martin? I've been thinking about laying it all down." John had studiously avoided the subject until he felt the time was right for dealing with it. There were still a number of bookings on his calendar, and his father, who was handling the dates and travel schedule, needed some answers soon. "I don't know if I can go through with those appearances."

The counselor–priest sipped his coffee and rocked in his chair with a trace of a smile on his lips. "Well, John, I can't tell you what to do. That's a decision only you can make. But I have some ideas which you may consider as advice, if you like."

"I'm ready."

"I hope so, because I believe you should think twice before hanging up your guitar. You have a very apparent gift from God in your music and it must be expressed appropriately. To quit now would be to hide the light God has given you. Remember the words of Jesus in his Sermon on the Mount: 'Let your light shine before men in such a way that they may see your good works, and glorify your Father who is in heaven.'[1]

"And there is another consideration perhaps just as important, if not more so. You may want to keep in touch with Protestant evangelical Christianity, instead of withdrawing from it. I think God has chosen you as a bridge builder, a force for unity in the tragically divided body of Christ." He paused. "It's just a thought. I don't want to push you, of course."

"Just pray about it, John. The Lord will point the way."

John responded with an all-telling, "hmmmmm," and pondered Fr. Martin's words as their eyes met in spiritual communication of the Word of God beyond words. John followed Fr. Martin's advice.

Once he had determined that he must follow through with his scheduled performances, John went out to face the crowds once again, bolstered by a revived spirit and a routine of daily prayer. His message was simple and Christ-centered, with an emphasis on worship. He was a wandering minstrel on a mission of love, with words of hope and encouragement.

He became known for his simple appearance. He had cut his hair from its customary waist-length to his shoulders. The word was out that John Talbot was undergoing some "heavy changes." But only a few knew what they really were.

"One of my main concerns during this period was for the church. I would go out across the land to sing in churches and was horrified at the fragmentation, the division between brothers. Every group had their own ideas about where the church was going and their own interpretation of the Bible—all different. Who was right? Someone had to be wrong. It seemed like such a scandal. I wondered where all these denominations and sub-denominational entities had come from, so I began earnestly to seek answers to these ecclesiastical questions, primarily through the study of church history," John relates. "All were good Christians, good willed, and well educated. What was the missing ingredient for unity in the church?" John concluded it had to be in the early church from which the scriptures were all quoted.

As he looked into the writings of primitive Christianity and the life of the early church he found that his anti-Catholic bias and Protestant ideas were shaken severely. His first realization was that there was an awful lot of history between the apostles and Luther, yet he had never been taught about those crucial centuries. He discovered that the most direct descendant of the early church was none other than Roman Catholicism and Orthodoxy, which traces its heritage back to the apostolic era. Once he had examined the Reformation, which fractured the church in the 1500s, he had to question his status as a Protestant. "Why should I protest?" he would ask.

What John found when he researched the archives of church history was not the contemporary Roman Catholic Church. However, he found in the early church the seed that possessed all the potential and promise of the Catholic faith we know today. One of the central features of John's faith, and what he had come to view as his final authority as an evangelical Protestant Christian, was the Bible. Now he discovered that the Scriptures were not even codified into what we now call our Bible until several hundred years after Christ, through a process of canonization, which, from time to time, included different groups of writings until the present configuration evolved. A definitive list of books did not fully appear until Luther challenged the authority of the book of James, as well as the seven extra books called the, "Apocrypha," or the "Deutero-Canonical" books. The Council of Trent formally established the books in the bible, based on the whole tradition leading up to it.. This took place within the Catholic Church.

The Scriptures

The scriptures came out of the life of the early Church. They were assembled by the authority of God established in that same Church. So if we deny the authority of the Church, we deny the authority of scripture. Then we are lost, for as St. Jerome said, "Ignorance of scripture is ignorance of Christ."

If there is a debatable passage of scripture today (and I think that there are a few!) it only makes sense to go back to the early Church from which they came to see if they had a substantial agreement on the interpretation of that same scripture. Then we can apply that interpretation to our situation today in a developed way.

How? We find that interpretation in the early Church fathers. Who? I found the primitive expression of Catholicism in the Didache (The Teaching of the Twelve Apostles), Clement of Rome's Letter to the Corinthians, Ignatius of Antioch's letters to the churches, Iranaeus of Lyons, Tertullian's writings from his orthodox period, Justin Martyr, and Cyprian of Carthage. There are many more. The earlier writings are easy and fun, but most challenging to read, for they are written in a very biblical style.

What is challenging to the non-Catholic reader of the Fathers is that all of the debatable beliefs and practices of Roman Catholicism are clearly in place, albeit in a primitive form. The divinity and humanity of Jesus (The Hypostatic Union), the Trinity, the special role of Mary in the Incarnation, apostolic succession in the bishops and the primary role of the bishop of Rome, the Eucharist, the communion of saints, purgatory. The list is well known among non-Catholic apologists, but the early Church is often overlooked.

It was from this process of study that I came to find the teachings of the Roman Catholic Church in the early Church, and their clear focus on one simple and profound point: the person of Jesus, and our personal love relationship with Jesus as a united people of God. All Catholic teaching revolves around this concept. Any doctrine, sacrament, or church structure that is not focused on this on one way or another is vain, and fruitless. But I found that all Catholic teaching immediate, or at least eventually, finds its way back to this central reality.

Today this is seen in the Catholic teaching that three things are needed for God's authority in ordinary teaching: Scripture, Tradition, and Magisterium. To have living authority

Scripture needs to be interpreted, or fleshed out in the Church, through Tradition. To give a unified interpretation of Tradition we need Magisterium, or the teaching authority of the Church. The Protestants are a clear example of those who try to go with Scripture alone, and end in fractured disunity. The Orthodox and Anglicans use Scripture and Tradition, but still end up divided from each other without a clear leader evidenced in Scripture, Tradition and Philosophical Common Sense. Catholics might still be divided on interpretation of some things, but at least we do so from the position of unity regarding greater things. I love the monastic life and the Liturgy in the Orthodox communities and churches, but as I studied the Orthodox and the Catholics, I began to see the greater wisdom of the Roman Catholic position. Though I love many things (the love of scripture, and the fellowship) in the Protestant tradition, it had ceased to be a credible option by this time.

So I was being confronted with the reality of the Catholic Church on two levels: My head was being challenged through the study of Patristics, and my heart was being challenged by the wealth of the Church's contemplative and mystical tradition.

I was also being confronted with the radical gospel living that was central to the entire monastic, Franciscan, and consecrated life tradition. The Church has always encouraged such radicalism (not fanaticism) when those desiring to live the gospel radically do so with a truly humble attitude and spirit within the context of the wider Church universal. ⌒ JMT

"My questions of authority were answered as I looked at the formation of the Scriptures," John states. "The authority of the Scriptures was established through the God-given living authority of the early church, through its leadership, lifestyle, and worship. God's own authority of the Scriptures comes through the authority of the Church—and not the other way around, as many believe. If we negate the authority of the very Church that authorized the Bible, we also inadvertently negate the authority of the Bible itself. I recognized that most fundamentalists and evangelicals see the Bible as their 'final authority' while denying the authority of the Catholic Church, through which God gave us the Scriptures. The result, of course, is that they unknowingly end up denying the very authority of the Bible that they are trying to prove."

John also launched into a study of the early church fathers. "I found the early church to be Catholic," John asserts with conviction. "It is an undeniable historical fact. I had to start asking myself some pretty serious questions about what I would do about my findings. I was beginning to identify very strongly with the Catholic Church, which went against everything I had been raised with as a Protestant."

The Place of Peter

Ignatius of Antioch, who was one of the primary early Church leaders, referred to the Roman Church as the one "which holds the presidency" among other churches. And Saint Iranaeus of Lyons (A.D. 140–202) said the church in Rome played a powerful role. He called it, "the greatest and most ancient church known to all... that church which has the tradition of the faith which comes down to us after having been announced to men by the apostles. For with this church, because of its superior origin, all churches must agree." By around A.D. 200, Tertullian was calling the bishop of Rome the "Vicar of Christ," who was seen as the keeper of unity and truth.

Around A.D. 250, Saint Cyprian of Carthage wrote, "There is one God and one Christ and one church and one chair founded on Peter by the word of the Lord. It is not possible to set up another altar or . . . another priesthood."

Soon, the church began calling the bishop of Rome the Pope, a term which may sound formal and official to us, but which comes from the word, "papa."

⟶ From *The Music of Creation* by John Michael Talbot

Then there was the important role of tradition within Catholicism. John was part of a generation that had made "tradition" a dirty word, along with other loaded terms, like "discipline," "establishment," and "patriotism." One great convert to Catholicism, the nineteenth-century English writer G.K. Chesterton, makes a strong case for the idea of tradition:

> Tradition means giving votes to the most obscure of all classes, our ancestors. It is of the dead. Tradition refuses to submit to the small and arrogant oligarchy of those who merely happen to be walking about. All democrats object to man being disqualified by the accident of their birth; tradition objects to their being disqualified by the accident of death....We will have the dead at our councils. The ancient Greeks voted by stones; these shall vote by tombstones.[11]

Certain questions still frightened John away from embracing the Catholic faith. What about the emphasis on Mary, papal infallibility, the endless repetition of liturgical worship, purgatory, prayer to the saints, confession, and ornate sanctuaries? And then there was transubstantiation, the belief that Christ is actually present in the Eucharist. These questions needed answering.

Over a period of time, John's hungry mind researched each

question with the care of a Swiss watchmaker, and the answers he found met the demanding criteria for authenticity set by his own skepticism. What he determined was that Catholicism, with all its ritual, liturgy, tradition, and devotional practices, is Christocentric, that is, Christ at the very heart of everything. If Mary is deemed important, it is only because Jesus, the fruit of her womb is far more important. If the saints are venerated, it is because Jesus is worshiped as God. The Eucharist honors not only his memory, as John had been taught in his evangelical days, but it produced his real presence for us, according to his words in John 6:3. Jesus is the *living bread*. John explains, "The Eucharist is the real presence of the paradoxes that Jesus actually is. It is the fullest sacramental expression of the Paschal Mystery." And these things obtain their value not by the capricious, arbitrary judgment of some archaic, dust-covered medieval church. They maintain their value by association; association with the crucified and risen Christ of history. In fact, John found that almost all of the seemingly complex practices and structures of the Catholic Church are rooted firmly in the simplicity of three basic concepts: the incarnation of Christ, the passion of Christ, and the giving of the Spirit of Christ to the church.

John discovered further that liturgical practices and sacred reading are based in ancient Jewish and early church customs, all of which have some deeper meaning and are based on written and oral traditions that share an overriding concern—to communicate the redemption of mankind, thematically spanning the ages from Adam's fall to the apocalypse and man's final judgment. Furthermore, John was developing a more sacramental understanding of life, seeing God working mystically and spiritually through the signs and symbols of the whole created world, now growing into full redemption in Christ. The hidden beauty of Catholicism filled him with wonder and excitement. His mind staggered under the growing realization that this was to be his church, his home in the body of Christ.

Sacrament and Mystery

The word, "sacrament" means "mystery," among other aspects of the definition. The sacraments symbolize a grace from God already at work in a person's life, but they also cause that grace to grow stronger. Catholics and most Orthodox Christians say that sacraments "symbolize and effect grace." They are also a way to enter into the mystery of our relationship with God through Christ. We use tangible elements of bread, wine, oil, and water, for instance, but through them they cause the intangible grace they symbolize to become a spiritual reality. This is true especially in the Eucharist, or what non-Catholics often call the Lord's Supper. Here, the early Church clearly understood that Jesus was mystically present in the Eucharist, simply because He told them it was true. Did they fully understand it? No, it was a mystery. But they knew it to be true simply because Jesus had said it (Jn. 6). It causes no less confusion today than it did when all but the disciples abandoned Jesus after this teaching! —— JMT

Another aspect of sacrament began to affect John Michael: If mystical reality occurs in the Sacraments, they also can occur in the normal activities of life. Through the 'stuff' of daily life, Jesus mystically appears. But it takes faith to see him. St. Francis said that if we see Jesus by faith in the natural reality of bread and wine, so can we see Jesus under the appearance of our brothers and sisters in Christ, and in every person on earth. This 'sacramental' way of seeing life is decidedly Catholic, and was transforming John's way of seeing everything!

This way of seeing natural things in a new light are sometimes called, "incarnational," or "in flesh, or meat." Jesus was the "Word made flesh." Likewise, John Michael was beginning to see all natural phenomenons as windows on the supernatural.

Once John Michael got past the Catholic/Protestant issues, he had to decide between Orthodoxy and Roman Catholicism. The two churches split, East and West, in 1054 AD over theological issues concerning the procession of the Holy Spirit in the Trinity, and more primarily over the politics of the center of the later Roman Empire. Orthodoxy would grant the Bishop of Rome a primacy of honor among the five ancient Patriarchies of Rome, Constantinople, Jerusalem, Antioch, and Alexandria. Rome interpreted that as actual and ongoing leadership over, and through those, Patriarchs in time of division and crises.

John Michael was strongly drawn to the Orthodox position. He loved their Liturgy, more rich in symbol, color, sound, and even taste and smell, but thought that the lengthy two to three hour service might become tedious on a regular basis. The Roman liturgies tended to be shorter, and starker by comparison. John especially had a leaning towards the monastic expressions of the Eastern churches. Without question the earliest expressions of the semi-eremitical and cenobitical monasticism John Michael came to love had its origins in the East. Even St. Benedict and St. Francis were highly influenced by the ancient expressions of the monastic East.

The deciding factor for John Michael came down to unity. Even though the Eastern churches claim a unity of spirit, they could not match the unity of the Roman Church. National and theological barriers existed so strongly that real division still plagues Orthodoxy. No other Christian expression, not to mention any religion on earth, could match the unity of Roman Catholicism. Plus, in that huge unity, there are places for just about everyone who wants to follow Jesus Christ in an orthodox way.

For John Michael the greatest argument for Roman Catholicism was the simple existence of the Pope, the Bishop of Rome. He is sought after and listened to like no other religious leader on earth. With some one billion Roman Catholics he is the leader of the single largest united religious community on earth. But the people would not be so united without the Peterine ministry of the Pope, and the Pope would not be so revered among believers and non-believers alike without the people. The two have worked together to produce the greatest argument for the Roman Catholic Church: the largest fully united religion on the face of the earth. No other expression of Christianity, no matter how ancient or well intended, has been able to so literally fulfill the teaching of Jesus regarding the unity of the Church.

Drawn to the Church

There were three things that really drew me into the Catholic Church: 1) the rich contemplative and mystical tradition, 2) the balance of scripture, tradition and magisterium (or the Church's teaching authority), 3) and the monastic heritage of radical gospel movements and communities. The first brought a depth that I could not find in Protestant and Evangelical Christianity, the second brought integrity and a unity to scripture and its interpretation in a united Church, and the third brought the possibility of the support of a radical gospel community to bring renewal to individual disciples and to the Church as a whole that is formally encouraged by the Church herself. These things spoke volumes to me about a time tested spiritual home in which to follow Jesus Christ more radically, without falling back into religious fanaticism and fundamentalism. ⌒ JMT

In the midst of this profound process of spiritual enlightenment, John went to Father Martin one day and announced that he would like to formally enter the Catholic Church. Father Martin just smiled at first. He was happy with John's determination to convert, but he issued a word of caution. "John Michael, I think it would be wise to wait, and let me tell you why I think so. You are a well-known musician. My guess is you will continue to gain in popularity around the country. But remember, these are Protestant brothers and sisters and they are going to have a lot of questions for you. They will put you to the test and you must be able to answer them in love, with authority, and with understanding. Remember our three guidelines for proving our faith: it must be scripturally, historically, and philosophically consistent. This will take a bit more study."

John's heart sank for a moment, but he submitted to his spiritual director's guidance. Besides, he knew there was much more to learn. He would welcome more time for catechetical studies. In particular, Fr. Martin had John read John Henry Newman's *Development of Christian Doctrine*.

Father Martin added a parting word. "You know, John, the Catholic Church is and has always been made up of human beings who make mistakes. Take, for example the corruption of the medieval era. You can be sure there will be those who will challenge you on the basis of some of the darker chapters in Catholic history. Like God's beloved chosen people, Israel, we have sinned, we have fallen, and we have been tragically unfaithful at times. But we are His—we are redeemed. So, my young friend, in the words of the Apostle Paul, I would exhort you to 'Study, to show yourself approved.'"

John took heart at his mentor's words of wisdom. He would have to forge his understanding and knowledge in such a way as to articulate his faith lovingly and incontrovertibly, compassionately and convincingly. He found that he could identify closely with those Roman centurions who are said to have converted to Judaism. They recognized the Jews to be the people of God, and Judaism to be the way of salvation. They would encounter the stumbling blocks of religious bureaucracy, temple harlots, corrupt priests, and cynical religious leaders.

But through it all they saw the God of redemption, were bathed in the baptism of the mikva, endured the pain of circumcision and faced the ridicule of their contemporaries. John felt much the same, and he drew strength from the words that God whispered quietly in his soul: "John, I want you to become a Catholic. This church has suffered, become ill, and, at times, has very nearly died, but she is My first church, and today I am breathing new life into her. You will be part of this renewal."

Walk through the Liturgy and Eucharist

At the beginning of my Catholic experience I found the Liturgy a marvelous way to give some structure to common and private prayer using scripture and patristic writings as texts. There are many modern attempts to do this, but I figured, why reinvent the wheel? All of the work has been done, so why not reap the benefits of the heartfelt work of so many saints and scholars, both of which I am not? So the Liturgy, especially the Liturgy of the Hours and the Eucharistic Liturgy's readings and ancient prayers, became a great tool for personal growth, and a traditional way to structure our new community's common prayer times throughout the day.

Later the Liturgy began to significantly deepen for me. First, I was aware that liturgical prayer is greater than either my private prayer, or the common prayers of a particular community. It is literally the prayer of the entire Church. Because of this the early Church believed that the angels and the saints were mystically present during the praying of the Liturgy. St. Benedict mentions that God is present everywhere, but is especially present during the Liturgy. This is an awesome reality to contemplate during Liturgical prayer.

As the years passed I gradually sank deeper and deeper into the Liturgy. The day in and day out recitation of the scriptures had caused them to become second nature to me. It was even beyond memorization. They intuitively became a part of my very being in God.

I also realized that, at a time when "Liturgy Practice" is becoming so popular among Buddhists, we have the same thing in Christ and the Church, just as ancient, if not more so.

In recent years I have discovered what I call a "walk through the liturgy" at every liturgy. It involves a sinking from the external and knowable realities of the Faith, to that which can only be known through pure spiritual intuition, or what the mystics call "unknowing". We begin with the external things of the senses and passions of the body in liturgical use of sacred place, sights, sounds, smell and touch through the use of religious art, sacramentals and ritual, and so on. The entrance Hymn and Penitential Rite use the senses of the body to stir the emotions in a positive way as preparation for further journey in Christ through the rest of the liturgy.

Next comes the Liturgy of the Word, including scripture readings and a homily by a duly ordained or appointed clerical or lay minister. This stirs the spiritual mind, or what the masters call the soul. This is more than just a logical grasp of scripture or Church teaching. It is mystical in its presentation, and in its hearing, for those who have the faith to perceive this mystery.

Last comes the Liturgy of the Eucharist. Here we move from the knowable things of senses, passions, and the mind, to the deeper knowing of God through complete mystery and spiritual intuition. This is true rebirth and awakening in Christ. Once this place of mystery in discovered, then all else becomes transformed in this miracle. Every action, every emotion, and every word become sacred vehicles for awakening and spiritual rebirth in Christ through the Liturgy. Once this is awakened, then every thought, emotion, action and word of every moment and relationship in life become reborn in the rebirth of Christ. All becomes a miracle.

Related to this was my deeper appreciation of the Eucha-

rist. At the beginning of my Catholic experience I certainly loved the Eucharist, and accepted it as an ongoing miracle instituted by Christ for the faithful of every age. But it took years to develop into something more wonderful and rich in my personal experience of the Faith. With the day-in and day-out celebration and reception of this wonder of wonders, something began to really change within me. The realities I accepted about the Eucharist as a convert to Roman Catholicism began to intuitively take up residence in my deepest soul and spirit.

Often I would go to a Mass, and the people were down right unfriendly, the music was awful, and the preaching was anything but inspirational. Yet, once I received Jesus in the Eucharist the complete mystical reality of the Catholic Christian faith became a miraculous spiritual intuition that overwhelmed my whole being, spirit, soul, and body. Everything about faith in Jesus Christ and life in the Church is intuitionally received in the reception of what appears only to be a thin wafer of bread, and a sip of wine. But it is really the Body and Blood of Jesus Christ, who created the world, and established the Church to which I now belonged. Once received, then I saw the entire Church, and the entire world in a new miraculous and reborn manner. Suddenly, it did not matter as much about the unfriendly people, or the bad preaching and music. Once I discovered this inner personal freedom, I was less apt to try to change externals of the Church for my own benefit. I was more able to really do something in Christ to fix the problem from a place of interior rebirth without condemning the attempts of faith by others. Plus, once I changed it seemed that people suddenly became friendlier, and the music and preaching became better. Yet they had not changed, I had changed interiorly, and now all externals found a healthy place. The same thing happened in my relationships and work in community and family.

~ JMT

So he continued his studies for another six months, after which time Father Martin and a small company of Franciscan friends and relatives received him into the Roman Catholic Church on Ash Wednesday, 1978. He had come to believe that everything he had learned pointed him toward Rome. John's overwhelming experience was similar to that of Chesterton, who wrote:

It is very hard for a man to defend anything of which he is entirely convinced. It is comparatively easy when he is only partially convinced. He is partially convinced because he has found this or that proof of the thing, and he can expound it. But a man is not really convinced of a philosophic theory when he finds that *something* proves it. He is only really convinced when he finds that *everything* proves it. And the more converging reasons he finds pointing to this conviction, the more bewildered he is if asked suddenly to sum them up. [4]

John found that the whole case for Catholicism is that the case is both extremely simple and very comprehensive. The very multiplicity of proofs, which should make his argument overwhelmingly convincing, makes it nearly impossible. This was just another of the many paradoxes he would discover along the way. It was as though a veil had fallen from his startled spiritual eyes. For so long he had viewed the Catholic "cathedral" from the outside, seeing only its cracked bricks and weather-beaten façade, totally ignorant of the wondrous beauty of its sculpted interior—a hidden treasure that now was his through the rich inheritance of his adoption by the Mother Church.

Evangelical and Protestant Churches

For me the Evangelical and Protestant expressions of Christianity were not bad, they were just incomplete. I describe them (for better or worse) as great line drawings of Christ. The lines are in all of the right places, and, as pencil drawings are even quite expressive. For the artist, we know that this is an art form unto itself. But I hungered for the rich oil painting of Jesus, with all of the subtle, deep tones, and expressive hues. For me, Catholic Christianity brought greater life-likeness to the spiritual painting of my life.

I have often said that, though I truly love the Evangelical and Protestant traditions, I would find it most difficult to go back. Based on the promise to the Church that "the gates of hell shall not prevail against" the Church, built on and protected with the keys of the kingdom given by Christ to St. Peter, I cannot imagine ever leaving the Church. If I did, I would probably end up some generic Buddhist/Taoist/Hindu maintaining a great love for Jesus. I would have cut myself off from the rich historical stream of apostolic tradition that brings humanity any sure record of Christ in the first place. Without the Church there can be no authoritative scripture, which is the earliest written account of apostolic tradition regarding Jesus Christ and the Church. I could never deny my love for Jesus, but I would at that point be unable to profess a historic faith in Jesus. So, it is either the Catholic Faith or nothing when it comes to any orthodox expression of the Christian Faith.

〜 JMT

"I will never forget that day," John asserts. "I was received with the rites of initiation, including conditional baptism. My godparents, Chuck and Ellen Callahan, provided a small flask of water brought all the way from the Jordan River. It was a very moving experience."

"I remember one friar, Fr. Anton, with a very dry sense of humor. We were still using the old rite with water, salt, and chrism oil. Fr. Anton looked at the elements on the altar for a long time, began to smile wryly, turned to me and said, 'If this don't take, nothin' will!' More seriously, when word got around that I was going to be confirmed that night another friar, Fr. Maury (who was usually somewhat irreverent), stopped John, who was busy getting things ready hours before the ceremony, and said, "You should be in the chapel praying." John went right to the chapel and began to pray.

John's parents were in attendance and watched the proceedings with great interest. Within a year they would follow their youngest child into the Church. When asked whether John's experience had influenced her, Jamie responded with an unexpected answer. "Johnny was always such an extremist—I wouldn't be budged by his enthusiasm. I suppose you could say that I became a Catholic in spite of John. He left some of his

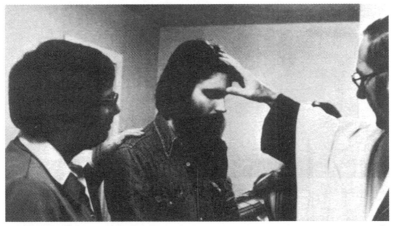

John's Conditional Baptism, Confirmation, and First Communion on Ash Wednesday, 1978 at Alverna's upper Room Chapel. Fr. Martin Wolter (right) receives John into the Roman Catholic Church, as friend and sponsor, Chuck Callahan looks on.

theology books lying around and I began reading them. I wanted to find a church home and was convinced, after studying the origins and development of the Catholic Church, that this was it. Three months later I was confirmed."

Jamie also noted her childhood baptism by their Catholic neighbor. It seems the sacramental mark of this experience had pursued her throughout her life. By this time, the entire family had converted, with the exception of Terry.

And how did this experience affect big brother? "I was very happy for John," Terry says. "His Catholicism has been wonderful for him. I had always trusted him intellectually, and his experience helped me understand a lot of things, too." Although they disagreed on certain theological issues, the brothers shared a relationship that served as an ecumenical ideal, transcending old barriers and isolation by capitalizing on the central issues of their faith. They based their relationship upon the rock of the Gospel message: Love.

"One of the themes of my ministry is integration: healing and reconciliation ... unity," John states with great emphasis. " 'In my house are many mansions,' Jesus said. There are many expressions of Christian faith and I will not judge any of them. Instead, we must regather, come together into a building made of living stones—the church of Jesus Christ—sharing all our marvelously diverse gifts and personalities. Yes, I believe we are one in Christ already, but we must continue to unify, to direct our hearts and minds toward reconciliation."

Keith Green

I knew Keith from the earliest days in Christian music. We had a rather turbulent relationship, but I loved him like a brother. We were both idealists, were both quite strong-willed.

Keith and I met when we played together in the studio on the Jamie Owens Growing Pains *project, produced by Al*

Perkins of the Flying Burrito Brothers, and my older brother. I was on acoustic guitar, Keith on keyboards, Lee Sklarr on bass, and a guy named "Pooh Bear" on drums. From the start Keith didn't seem to like me, yet I think he always wanted me to like him. I was trying to eat healthy, but he informed me that I would go to hell if I wouldn't eat at Mac Donald's. This relationship was not off to a great start.

My next encounter with Keith was at Knotts Berry Farm for a Christian music day. Barry McGuire was the headliner, with the Talbot Brothers next, and Keith as the opening act. That night he took the stage, and didn't leave until after everyone else's time had expired. It was simply outrageous, so things were a bit tense back in the dressing room. When we asked him why he was so arrogant, he said it was the will of God, and that he was the anointed one for that night. We were not impressed.

I next butted heads with Keith after his first album was just released and was getting some serious notice. He was playing at a small theatre in Indianapolis. By that time I had moved to Alverna, and was trying to put my shattered Christian life back together. I went to see Keith at the concert, and afterwards, he abruptly accused me of leaving my wife to become a monk. He again reminded me that I was going to hell.

Then came the infamous Catholic Chronicles. Keith called me to tell me that he was writing them, and asked my opinion. I told him that a constructively critical tract would be good, to challenge Catholics to live their faith more radically for Christ, and that he should seek the input of some great Catholic evangelists and scripture scholars. He chose not to follow my advice, and wrote a highly critical tract based on weary old proofs that neither Catholics nor Protestants take seriously. They did much harm to those who did not know the Bible, or their own Catholic faith. Many Catholics and Protestants tried to get Keith to stop, but he refused.

> *Not long after that Keith and two of his children, Josiah and Bethany, died in a tragic plane crash taking off from an airstrip nearby the Last Days Community in Texas. I was deeply saddened at his death, and that we had never reconciled.*
>
> *Years later, his widow, Melody Green, came to our community in Arkansas and humbly requested forgiveness on behalf of Keith and their community. I knew that this humility embodied the deeper spirit of Keith Green. We prayerfully and tearfully reconciled that day, and Melody holds my utmost respect to this day.* ⁓ JMT

It was more than coincidence that John's baptism, confirmation and first communion were administered on Ash Wednesday, the beginning of the forty-day Lenten period of penance, self-denial, and introspection that precedes Easter. Lent is a time for letting worldly things fall away in favor of drawing closer to Christ. Indeed, John was to follow the example of a man known as history's most penitent of all Christian pilgrims, one who would renew the church with his tears, his prayers, his songs, and his wounds, after the example of Jesus Christ himself. His name was Giovanni Francesco Bernardone; he is known more widely as Saint Francis of Assisi. Through Francis John would discover the beauty and the penitential way of all of the monastic and patristic saints.

John was to begin a Catholic vocation that would be filled with opportunities for comfort, trials, and penance. Indeed, St. Benedict wrote in his monastic rule that the monk's life is to be a perpetual Lent. If John had known what still lay ahead, he would have been filled with trepidation and fear, and fallen on his face in prayer for the mercy and grace of God. His being received into the Catholic Church on Ash Wednesday instead of Easter was a prophetic sign of John Michael's religious life.

Holy Man in the Woods

July 3, 1978

> God has revealed some definite direction for me to follow vocationally this past week. I heard Jesus tell me to open my Bible for further guidance. I immediately opened to Mark 10:21, and Jesus' words again were, "There is one thing more you must do. Go and sell what you have and give to the poor; you will then have treasure in heaven. After that, come and follow me."
>
> The words need no explanation. Now I wait to follow the call of Jesus. I believe God wants me to set up a community called "Charity" to fulfill the vision he gave me of a community that was like a beautiful painting of harmony. I believe God wants me to give all my possessions to this community to fulfill his word for me to free myself from all material ownership. I believe God wants me to enter the Third Order of St. Francis and live as a contemplative hermit to fulfill the vision of my apostolate.
>
> ⁓ From *Changes* by John Michael Talbot

Who was Saint Francis of Assisi? There can be no true understanding of John Michael Talbot's life and ministry without some insight into the one after whom John has patterned his life. It's not that John desired to displace Jesus Christ as his supreme model of faith, but rather that Saint Francis achieved, in John's eyes, perhaps more than any other person, conformity to the image of Christ. Saint Paul urged believers to "be imitators of me, as I am of Christ," and on this principle, an international movement of Christian "imitators," the Franciscans, arose to follow the example of Saint Francis, a poor beggar dressed in rags who preached a Gospel of love that was to shake Christian Europe to its foundations.

Saint Francis is the patron saint of Italy, of animals, of ecology, and perhaps most importantly in our age of nuclear weapons, he is the patron saint of peace. He forbade his followers to bear arms. His artistic talents helped provide impetus to the Renaissance and it has been said that his "Canticle of Brother Sun" was the earliest major poem penned in the Italian language. Franciscan missionaries carried the Gospel to China, and even sailed with Columbus. Major cities, mountain ranges, rivers, and geographic regions bear his name, not to mention many great institutions around the world. Of special significance since terrorists attacked the US on September the 11th, 2001, are the interfaith meetings for peace called by Pope John Paul II in Assisi, the town of St. Francis. This was done under the patronage of St. Francis of Assisi.

It was in the early 1200's, in the days of Pope Innocent III that the neighboring cities of Perugia and Assisi teetered on the brink of war. It was all over money, who could make it and who controlled it. Under the Feudal system the upper class, called "majors," or the "maggiore," controlled a town. Most trade was done by barter, with money only being used as an auxiliary means. The lower class, the "minors," or "minore," had no control over the socio-economic, or political system in which they lived, worked, and died. They felt like slaves. This class system was passed from one generation to the next. The people finally began to rise up. A new capitalism was sweeping across Europe. With it, money was used as the primary means of trade, and the minors, the poor working class, could work themselves out of the lower class through hard labor. They could become the maggiore, the wealthy upper class. They also elected some of their civil officials.

In Assisi the people overthrew the old Feudal system, and opted for capitalism and democracy. They stormed the Rocca Maggiore, or the Castle of the Rich with nothing but farm tools and their bare hands, fought the armed guards, gained victory, and began to dismantle the fortress one rock at a time. The town, and the whole country, was wild with desire for the new capitalism and democracy as a means to true happiness. Francis' father, Pietro Bernardone, took full advantage of this new opportunity and became very wealthy through the cloth trade. He even married into the French upper class with Lady Pica, the kindly mother of St. Francis.

Francis saw through the false promise of mere external pleasure of wealth and prestige, no matter how legitimate the better political system might seem, and gave it all up to follow Jesus, the real way to happiness for humanity. Not only did he refuse to use the newest means of wealth in money, he also refused to be called anything but a minor, a lower class citizen. It would be like refusing to use credit cards and computers today. This upset Francis' father, and many of the fathers of the youths who came to join Francis in those earlier years.

Francis had initially graduated from partying to soldiering as hostilities between the two cities escalated. Francis's dreams of victory and glory were dashed when he was taken prisoner. The slaughter of war, imprisonment, and a lingering illness changed the young man, and, in spite of a homecoming followed by festive celebration, Francis was never to be the same; later he would claim it was then that God had spoken to him. He publicly renounced his previous commitment to frivolity, high living, and wealth in a radical conversion to simplicity, poverty, and the Gospel.

Donning dark sackcloth with a length of rope for a belt, he wandered into the countryside with nothing save his burning drive to follow God, who had urged him in a vision to "rebuild my church" as he was praying before a crucifix at the ruins of the old church of San Damiano. Humbly taking the message to heart, Francis set about acquiring stones with which to rebuild the fallen structure. This reconstruction project foreshadowed the spiritual revival of the Western church that Francis was to inspire. Francis had the humility to literally follow the vision of God, and do the lowly manual labor of rebuilding a derelict and forgotten rural church that still belonged to the Benedictines. Because of this humble obedience, God saw him fit to do greater rebuilding in the Church universal.

His gentle revolution, however, would not go unchallenged. There would be the classic "conflict between living piety and church authority, between the enthusiasm of Pentecost and the rigidity of church law," as Karl Adam wrote.[1] But most of the conflict came from those who saw this new socio-economic change as a real political answer. It came from those who had become rich by taking advantage of this new system. It came from those who had the most to lose, especially those whose sons and daughters wanted to join Francis in his gentle revolution.

At the advice of the bishop of Assisi, Francis and his first band of followers withdrew to the Rieti valley to begin their hermitical life and itinerant ministry. Only later, after they gained respect for their holiness, did the elders of Assisi welcome them back. Today, the merchants of Assisi are sometimes called the "Fourth Order," because they have now discovered a way to actually profit from Saint Francis.

Francis was a societal dropout—a medieval counterculture type, who wandered the continent, preaching repentance and challenging the inflexible, petrified Roman Catholic Church of his day with a kind of dynamic power unheard of since the mighty wind of the Holy Spirit had blown in Jerusalem's upper room. A grassroots movement grew, leaving thousands wearing the simple brown habit that had come to identify Franciscan disciples by the time Francis died.

Among the numerous charismatic gifts and miraculous signs associated with this great saint are the stigmata—the wounds of Christ's crucifixion—that were emblazoned permanently on Francis's hands, feet, and side. Francis was a man of both great joy and deep sorrow. While it is true that carefree happiness and joy were a part of Francis's life, he also entered into the darkness and pain of Jesus' crucifixion, the marks of which he would bear for the rest of his life.

John Michael Talbot's earliest inclinations would seem to have cast him in the role of a Franciscan, and later in the image of an archetypical monk, long before he was ever aware that such an expression of spirituality existed. From his childhood moments of solitude in nature to his reading of the three Scripture passages that would propel him to the Franciscan Third Order, John's life is one of parallels, echoes, and images of the great troubadour himself—Saint Francis.

John is fascinated by Saint Francis's passion for simplicity. "Francis was a simple man with a simple faith. He once said 'Blessed is he who expects nothing, for he shall enjoy everything.' Simplicity and poverty may be seen to bear on the peace issue also because Francis believed that those who have possessions must also have weapons with which to defend them. This was typical of his logic. I have always longed for that kind of life—it doesn't mean that we ignore the very real complexities and responsibilities around us; it just means that centrally our lives are about the simple faith of the good news of Jesus Christ," John affirms. "The three Scripture passages that came to me very forcefully, moving me toward a truly simple lifestyle, were along the following lines: The first is the tale of the rich young man whose refusal to sell his earthly possessions occasioned the parable of the camel and the needle.[2] The second was the commandment to the disciples to take nothing with them on their journey, neither a staff, nor extra clothing, no money.[3] The third was that to follow Christ we must also carry his cross.[4] Not only did I embrace these ideas from the Scriptures as I received them, but they were very much a part of Francis's call," he points out.

St Francis has been called an archetype and a reformer of the hermitical life of the Desert Fathers, the cenobitical life of St. Pachomius and St. Benedict, and a culmination of the 11th century Camaldolese, Carthusian, and Cistercian reforms. While an uncompromising Roman Catholic Christian, the itinerant wanderers and mendicants of the Hindu Sannyasins and Buddhist monks and Bodhisattvas, and Taoist sages often find a great counterpart in the person of St. Francis. The historic interfaith meetings that were held in St. Francis' town of Assisi by Pope John Paul II symbolize this.

Initially, to compare the life of John Michael Talbot with that of Saint Francis is an intriguing exercise in seeing double. Both may be said to have lived the rags-to-riches story in reverse, and by choice. Both had tasted the fruits of worldly success, material possessions, and popularity. Certainly both individuals may be said to have had radical "Damascus Road" type conversions, followed by the initial disapproval of loved ones. The same three Scripture passages inspired their vocations, and these callings were similar in that they were poetically, lyrically, and musically oriented. Both men, while wearing habits and engaging in religious life, were actually laymen prophetically addressing the church in humility, seeking its renewal. John, like

Francis, shares an immense love of nature, identifying with it as a kind of sibling under God's parenthood. Each has had a reputation for flinging himself into his work with total commitment and tenacity. And both are known for maintaining ascetical routines without being gloomy or morose. In fact, both are very celebrative. Both men, physically and figuratively have built up the stones of the church in active lives balanced by regular periods of deep contemplative prayer.

Thus it is not surprising that John, in 1978 after studying the life of Francis, should have immediately wanted to "join up." John's Franciscanization, so to speak, transpired simultaneously with his Catholic conversion process. Under the watchful eye of Father Martin, he became a Third Order, or Secular Franciscan. In this act, John joined with other lay people, single and married, and diocesan clergy wishing to identify with the spirit, call, and rule of Saint Francis. His call to monastic life would come thereafter.

There are three orders of Saint Francis: the First Order, or the Order of Friars Minor, who are celibate, vowed men. The Second Order is comprised of cloistered nuns, or "Poor Clares," as they are sometimes called, after the first Franciscan sister. The Third Order is subdivided into vowed and non-vowed brothers and sisters, as well as married couples, and diocesan clergy, who seek to follow the example of the saint from Assisi, either in community or private homes. It is in the latter order that ripples of renewal are being felt throughout the land, as the timeliness and relevance of Francis's message strikes home in our day. John became very much involved in this process.

Sprouting from within the context of his Franciscan roots, John may be called a monk, a hermit, a new religious, and a penitent, all terms that are qualified by a set of criteria long-established within the tradition of the Roman Catholic Church. A monk is a solitary (one who is called to solitude, either communally or individually.) A hermit's life includes substantial, but not necessarily total, solitude and silence. The consecrated religious professes the "evangelical counsels" of poverty, chastity, and obedience, either by a vow or a promise, either in the traditional celibate form, or the family expression in newer communities. The penitent is a class or order of brothers or sisters living a consecrated life in the church. Penitents are not necessarily seculars or vowed religious, yet many are religious in that they profess the evangelical counsels, and a number of penitents are Secular Franciscans, which is simply a modern name for Franciscan Penitents. Within history these developed into what is now called the Secular Franciscans, and the Third Order Regular. The Third Order Regular comprises nearly 400 autonomous communities in the one Franciscan family. Sometimes this is called "Seraphic confusion!"

While the various classes and ecclesiological terms may baffle the neophyte, it is important to think in terms of the Gospel for which Saint Francis lived and poured out his life. The central theme is to follow Christ diligently, to be conformed to his image by his call to repentance and love.

As John began to embrace the Franciscan ideals at Alverna, he felt himself deeply and totally drawn, not only to saint Francis, but also to the entire monastic stream in the Church, and to an uncompromisingly Christian community today, an ideal he had held for years. As he struggled in prayer for a more focused picture of his vocational direction, it seemed that five distinct ideas, some of which had been in the back of his mind since 1972, had begun to crystallize: an agrarian-based, substantially self-supporting prayer community; a call to poverty; a commitment to celibacy; a call to enter the Catholic Church, and a visual image of an old and tattered habit. One by one, these aspects of his spiritual odyssey had taken shape and were in various stages of development. He sought the advice of Father Martin on these matters, as he considered his suitability for the First Order of Saint Francis.

"John had a lot of questions when he first came to Alverna," Father Martin remembers. "His was a somewhat unusual situation and I took great interest in him from the beginning. His attraction to the church was from two angles: his attraction to Catholicism and his zeal to know more about Saint Francis. He fit the Franciscan ideal perfectly because of his sincere desire for simplicity, poverty, and humility. John has a unique talent, special graces. He is attuned to the new flow in the church—he has an uncanny feel for the times and seasons, so to speak. He bridges the gap between Protestantism and Catholicism, having tasted the best of both worlds: the born-again, emotional experience common to evangelicals, and the structured, liturgical disciplines of Catholic faith. He has heart and structure and a sense of how renewal is happening in both areas."

As John sought the wisdom of the priest regarding entry into the First Order, Father Martin advised him to move toward the Third Order instead. "The First Order is a much tighter institutionalized discipline—you'll find your wings clipped. You wouldn't be the free spirit you have been, which I feel is part of who you are," the priest cautioned during one of their many meetings. Actually, the community John founded became a reform of consecrated life, calling its members to an even more intense discipline of poverty and prayer. This would have been difficult to undertake from the ranks of the more lax, yet more institutional First Order.

John took to heart Father Martin's counsel and his suggestion to read about the life of Franciscan layman Raymond Lull. That this suggestion was made on the feast day of Lull added force to the idea of researching his story.

Raymond Lull was a married man who, after seeing a vision of Saint Francis, underwent a profound conversion experience with an accompanying desire to live a Franciscan lifestyle. After having lived of the high life, his new commitment to personal poverty and radically changed values were too much for his wife. He made provisions for his family's needs, lived as a hermit for a period of time, and then moved on to start contemplative Franciscan communities that served as training grounds for evangelists. He later took the Gospel to the Islamic world, pioneering this kind of evangelism in the Middle East, where he died. Lull became known as the prime example of Franciscan foreign missionaries, as the followers of Francis sought to take the Gospel of Jesus Christ to the four corners of the earth. Ironically, while it was the First Order friars who fulfilled this ambitious world mission, it was the Third Order, an order which some might be tempted to overlook, to which Raymond Lull belonged.

John took the advice and the example of Lull seriously and decided to become a Third Order Franciscan. He put on a ragged habit, walking yet another mile in his journey, fulfilling one more facet of his dream. Determining that it was time to withdraw temporarily from active life, John heeded an inner call to silence, solitude, and contemplation. He was about to embark on a trek into the wilderness to be tested, tempered, and tried.

November 8, 1978

I have sewn the habit of the vision this past day. It is made of second-hand army blankets I acquired from an army surplus store. I must say that I feel very comfortable in it, even though it is alien to all my cultural conditioning, and I am sure this is the habit of the vision. I now seek only the blessing of the provincial and the Alverna community.

I simply seek to be who I am and to follow God's call for me in childlike simplicity. I hope that in taking this habit I am doing only this.

    ~ From *Changes* by John Michael Talbot

During this time, John Michael would give something else up to a higher power. This time it was the life of his father. While John was in recording sessions for *The Lord's Supper* and *The Painter*, Dick became seriously ill. He had already had a bout with heart disease in the early 70s. A chain-smoker, he developed severe emphysema and heart problems. He checked into St. Vincent's in Indianapolis for a routine check up. During his stay he had a serious attack after dinner, aspirated, and went 6 minutes without breathing. The medical team resuscitated him, but his prognosis was not good. He hung between life and death for six weeks in intensive care. Later he was brought back into regular hospital care in a standard room.

October 9, 1978

> *My dad has nearly died several times since October 4th. His heart has failed. His lungs have failed. It is possible that his mind has failed as well. I cannot describe what I am experiencing. I feel as if I am dying so that he might be healed. I am downcast in hopes of his uplifting in Jesus. I feel as if I would take his sickness if only Jesus would heal him and bring him peace. In this I join with the sacrifice of Jesus. I pray that in this my father may be resurrected and healed.*
> — From *Changes* by John Michael Talbot

John Michael got the news while in a studio in downtown Indianapolis. They said that his father would probably not live through the night. "To say the least, it was a speedy drive out to the hospital on the northwest side of town. I passed cars on the right shoulder in order to get there before he might die. But he didn't die. God still had plans for him," John remembers.

After that, Dick went home to live out the remainder of his days, unable to walk down the hall without oxygen. He needed assistance in even the most basic functions of daily life. He had gone from a very self-reliant man of the World War II generation to being an invalid in a matter of months.

Some said the situation was tragic. But for John's father this time became a blessing. During his remaining days he discovered that he needed God in his life in a more serious way. He realized that every breath of air, every moment with a loved one was a precious gift from God. He gave his life to Christ and marked it by becoming a Catholic Christian.

John remembers it vividly. "It was in the little hospital chapel at St. Vincent's. A few of us family and friends gathered. My dad was confirmed and received his First Communion there without much fanfare, pomp, or ceremony. But for my family it became a major turning point in our relationship with Dad. He now had the faith of a child of God, yet through that faith came to the greatest wisdom that can be found in life on earth. For the family we discovered a side to our father that we never knew before. He was vulnerable, loving, and wise. He was an example of faith in the face of tragedy that turns the tragedies of life into opportunities for blessing."

John wrote his first setting of Psalm 23 for his father's Confirmation. "I sang it in that small chapel, and later recorded it for *Come to the Quiet*. About a year later I sang it a capella through choking voice and tearful heart and eyes at his funeral Mass at St. Pius X in Indianapolis," John relates. "When I sing it in concert today I always remember my dad and his faith, and a lifetime of dedication to the happiness of his family. It becomes a call to turn our tragedies into opportunities of faith just like my dad did."

An important decision made in those days involved music. After much agonizing and many hours of prayer, John decided to revive his musical career. After having put Sparrow Records on hold following his first two Christian albums, he called Billy Ray Hearn to push ahead with an ambitious new project. Using

1978 –
John Michael
was writing
*The Lord's
Supper*
during this
time.

the Catholic mass, and particularly the Eucharist as central themes, he wrote and recorded what became one of his biggest-selling albums, *The Lord's Supper*. He had given it all up, but God was about to deal it back to him. The album was a huge hit among Protestants and Catholics across the nation. After having made a promise to live in poverty, John's royalties would rapidly reach six figures (which was a lot in those days!)

What would he do with the money? How could he offer it to the Lord? Memories of Eureka Springs danced through his mind and his excitement rose.

Before a new dream could be realized, however, there was a more pressing matter—his desire to experience the rigors of the life of silence and solitude. John's initial consideration, and what was probably his most conscious motivation, was his sincere desire to truly be like the very early followers of Saint Francis, who dedicated themselves to prayer and radical simplicity.

"I was reading about their devotion, their prayers lives, and I said, 'Hey, why can't somebody just do it?" I felt an inner call to solitude—a time of separation to consider this lifestyle in more depth. I saw it as seeking and fulfilling the vision of solitude and simplicity all at once," he explained. "Just after I completed *The Lord's Supper* I retired to the woods."

The Lord's Supper and the Painter/Phil Perkins

As I settled into Alverna, I got used to living alone (which I had never done before), and I began to experience the rhythm of a liturgical day with the friars. It was at this time that new music began to emerge. It began as I read the missal that contained the words of the Mass. As I did so, words jumped out as being very singable, and easy to organize into verse and chorus. Soon songs were coming out as fast as I could sit down with my guitar to sing them. It was all rather spontaneous, and soon, the analogy of a painting began to emerge from a teaching I gave between songs in concerts.

I remember playing the songs for Terry during a joint concert we were doing in Fayetteville, Arkansas. Terry immediately told me that they were the best songs I had ever written, and were going to be something brand new for me. Neither of us could guess how right he was!

The Lord's Supper *was originally conceived as a double album called,* The Painter, Mass in the Key of D Major. *I recorded the entire body of songs at TRC recording in downtown Indianapolis. We originally tried putting drums and bass on after laying down the basic guitar and vocal, but it just didn't work, despite that being my usual process on two earlier Christian albums. We really didn't know what to do next.*

I had been listening to a lot of Gregorian chant in my room in the Carriage House at Alverna. I also appreciated the work of David Crosby with the Byrds, and Crosby, Stills, and Nash. Following these styles, I decided to use many layers of voices, far more than usual, on these new recordings. As I talked this through with Mark Clevenger, the engineer at TRC, Mark suggested that we try using singers from his new church, which was a new community integrating Orthodox and Western Charismatic spirituality. We agreed, and the sessions continued.

Immediately it became apparent that this would take hundreds of hours of overdubbing time in the studio. We used four to eight singers, and overdubbed them on every available track on a 24-track board, bounced it down to two tracks, and started again, then bounced down again until they had some 400 voices recorded. It was a laborious and time-consuming process.

The result was unlike anything we had heard before. It was choral, yet contemporary, classical, and yet charismatic. It was a musical expression of what I was going through spiritually and theologically as I inched my way into the Catholic Church, and what Mark's new community was going through as they became more Orthodox. It was a magical time to be in the studio. We knew that we were on to something very exciting and new.

Due to the lengthy recording process, and input from Billy Ray at Sparrow, they decided to split the material into two projects. One would be the parts of the Catholic Mass, to be released under a different name due to the non-Catholic CCM audience, and the other would contain the songs related to the analogy of the painting.

The mass parts were released as The Lord's Supper, and despite Sparrow's doubts about the project, it became a best seller. I soon began thinking about how to treat the remaining songs.

For years people had been asking Terry and me to get back together as the Talbot Brothers. I invited Terry to join me in the studio, and we soon found ourselves at TRC studio, where I had recorded The Lord's Supper. We tried a similar vocal approach using just our two voices, and it worked very well. The similarity of our voices, together with the outrageous *approach to multi tracking, caused our voices to become a choir, with each of us singing a part up to 100 times in the vocal booth.*

We just had great fun during those sessions. We spent as much time laughing as we did recording. We were having fun being brothers again, and doing the thing that we both loved most to do, making music. This attitude of fun became one of the earmarks of later sessions for Terry's projects as well. I guess we were sometimes more like the Marx Brothers than the Talbot Brothers!

Terry and I then took the project to London to add an orchestra. Billy Ray had met Lee Holdridge, who had worked with Neil Diamond, John Denver, and Barbara Streisand. When we arrived at the studio and heard the wonderful orchestrations, we knew that this had become something special. It had become bigger than either of us, so we just sat back and enjoyed the ride.

During that trip Terry and I spent a lot of time sightseeing in London. After years of separation, it was wonderful to enjoy being brothers again.

I also made another acquaintance during this time. Billy Ray had asked orchestral and choral arranger Phil Perkins to transcribe the vocal parts from The Lord's Supper *for choir. It was a daunting task, but after Phil got over the shock that I barely read music, we worked together for a few days, and put together a magnificent choral rendition of the whole work.*

Phil worked with me again on Come to the Quiet, *which began a string of successful collaborations on many more recordings and songbooks. Phil has become one of my closest lifelong friends, and has worked with me as orchestrator, arranger, and producer in most of my projects ever since. Relationships like that are hard to come by, and are worth more than money could ever buy.* — JMT

But there were also other forces in the realm of the Spirit that drove John to his decision to become a hermit. There was within him a deep thirst for the kind of wisdom that is not obtained from mortal men. There are shades of understanding and spiritual insight that may only be acquired through the shaping of the soul in a place of barrenness and total quiet. John knew that the history of the church offers many examples of monks who braved the wilderness alone to seek the face of God and his gifts of truth, produced like pearls in the hearts of those who truly live to discover. He wanted to share this experience.

Saint Benedict, a sixth-century Italian monk, was such a man. In his quest for God he established a monastic movement that would become the model for nearly all monastic life in the Western Church. Appropriately, he is called the father of Western monasticism. His biographer, Saint Gregory the Great, summed up Benedict's life with the phrase *soli Deo placere desiderans* ("he sought to please God alone"). He also said, "prefer nothing to Christ." Benedict's life was simple and austere.

History tells us that many have followed some form of the Benedictine Rule. John's awareness of the monastic tradition nudged him in that direction. It is still part of his spiritual core today. Of some interest to him were the cenobites, or community-based monks, such as the Benedictines and Cistercians. Of primary interest were the hermits, or solitaries, such as the Camaldolese and Carthusians. The call of the monk is, quite simply, the search for God alone. It is interesting to note that the earliest Franciscans were themselves hermits who mixed the contemplative life with the wandering life of the itinerant preacher. The "monastic body," according to the late Trappist monk Thomas Merton, "is held together not by human admirations and enthusiasms, which make men heroes and saints before their time, but on the sober truth, which accepts men exactly as they are in order to help them become what they ought to be."[5] This statement has the effect of putting the ideals of the monk within our grasp, and not reserved only for those spiritual giants who live alone in the cloistered cells of remote monasteries.

It seemed to John that, at least for him, God is not found in clamoring crowds or public places, but alone in the quietness of solitary thought and prayer. So he set about on a search for a place—a single cell or room in which he might escape the noise of the world and be captured in the grip of his God. The Scripture passage that kept ringing in his ears was in the words of Jesus himself, "Seek and you shall find; knock, and it shall be opened to you."[6]

One day, as he walked by the creek that runs through Alverna, he paused for a long moment at the Shrine to Our Lady of Lourdes with its beautiful statue of Mary. Fall was already in the air and a light mist hung just above the ground. He fixed his gaze on the image of the mother of Jesus. Except for the babble of the brook, there was silence. What about right here, he asked himself as his eyes fell upon a likely spot near the shrine. I'll build a hermitage with my own hands, just like Francis did at San Damiano, he resolved.

He made the following entry in his journal:

> I must now relate an incident that occurred on the feast day of Mary's assumption into heaven. I was walking along the ridge in the woods above the creek. I was engulfed into the being of these woods. I submerged myself in this hidden solitude to find God's presence in his creation. Soon I was led to the back of the shrine in honor of our Lady. It was there that I experienced incredible contemplative graces that surpass the mere words I would now use to describe them. It was upon this spot that I felt I had found my place of beginning. It was upon this spot that I felt I would be led to live my contemplative life in solitude.

John set about his task with single-minded perseverance; eyes riveted straight ahead to what Saint Paul called the mark of the high calling. Quietly but deliberately, he searched out the materials he would need to construct his chamber of prayer in the woods: an old barrel to serve as a wood burning stove, timbers with which to frame the structure, and stones to build it. "Like Francis," John wrote in his journal on August 24, 1978, "I will do lowly manual labor, not in exchange for money, but for the basics of food, clothing, and shelter."

During this time, Fr. Martin and the friars at Alverna put John through an informal novitiate. Fr. Martin directed his voluminous study. The other friars tested his sincerity and humility. They would humiliate him publicly. One habitually called him the "rent a monk" in front of retreatants. Another criticized his skill in the building of his hermitage. "They wanted to see if I would get angry and give up," says John today. He began to see both the gross and the subtle sins of the friars on a daily basis. He saw the "underbelly" of the church. Could he still see the perfect work of God in an imperfect Church and monastic Franciscan family? John Michael persevered.

"Friars, monks, and clerics are completely human people who are just seeking to follow God's call in an intentionally more intense way of life. Some have battles with alcohol or drugs, some with sexual issues, and many more with ordinary problems related to material pleasures and self will. In this they are like most everyone else. However, the way of life they have chosen remains very intense and sacrificial," John says today, after much experience. "Despite these very human trials, consecrated life is to be commended and encouraged for those who hear the call of God in that direction."

Precedents for facing the ravages of temptation in the wilderness predate Saint Benedict, and even Jesus. While they endured their fasting and solitude, the biblical prophets also sojourned in the desert, their greatest miracles of faith occurring in this stark environment. The ravens fed Elijah in the desert, and David exiled himself to the desert before ascending the throne. And long before these events, the Israelites, when called by God out of their slavery in Egypt (the bondage of sin) to pass through the waters of the Red Sea (baptism) on their journey to the Promised Land (the completed work of redemption), spent an entire generation in the desert, where they were tested, taught, and given the Ten Commandments. The desert wilderness, it would seem clear from the pattern, is an unavoidable link between the call to conversion and the call to vocation. The difference to be found among the redeemed is that they are the ones who have sought that place with holy determination, while others try to avoid it.

December 20, 1978

> *Well, it has begun. The hermitage is built, the habit is made, and they have both been blessed by God and by Father Martin. We had a lovely dedication Mass down here several days ago. I felt the special presence of God. It was good. I have also played my last concert for quite some time. I cannot describe how good it feels to get away from the materialistic and negative gossip that goes on in the Christian contemporary music ministry. I look forward to working from an ecumenical Catholic base that is well balanced and tested with time.* ⟿ From *Changes* by John Michael Talbot

When he completed his dwelling, John closed himself up like Noah in the ark until such time as God himself would summon him forth to an active life. Entombed for months on the hillside near the statue of the Virgin, cycles of contemplation, meditative prayer, and study were his daily lot, which also included a meager diet and an occasional walk through the woods.

"I felt as though I had been led by the Spirit into a wasteland to be tempted by the devil himself. And I was. The experiences that took place within me, and within that hermitage, I could never describe in words," John claims in a solemn tone. "I was brutally confronted with the horror of my own sinfulness, frailty, and susceptibility to temptation. In a very real way I was forced to deal with my own humanity, my mortality. It was an awesome experience."

December 30, 1978
The Development of Christian Doctrine and Life

I just walked and prayed by the creek. It was raining. I learned another lesson. The stream always changes. There is not one day, or even one hour, when the stream doesn't change. Sometimes it looks cold, other times it looks like a tropical swamp. I mean the "look" of the water. Not the color or the clearness. I mean the actual texture of the water. It is as we should be. Ever constant ... ever changing. The currents change as well. The creek bed also constantly changes. The shoreline is in a constant state of change. It is amazing how we think of it always the same, when it is never the same. Only its power and its presence are constant. Again, we should be like the creek. The love and the presence of Jesus should remain constant in our lives, yet the specifics of how we apply his love each day should always be open to change. This is the way of the creation of God. It should be the way of God's people as well. Then will we overcome the obstacles in our life, just as the stream eventually overcomes its obstacles as well. The creek has taught me much.

~ From Changes *by John Michael Talbot*

John was ready to live in the little hut for the rest of his life if God so directed. He would continue to read, write, and search out the mysteries of God. Ideas came forth as he considered his conversion and vocation, and he recorded them in his journal. Regarding concerts, he wrote, "They came to hear powerful oratories and I told them of silence. They came to hear my theological explanations of the Word and I simply shared with them my relationship with the living Word." Regarding prayer, "it is the foundation of life for the contemplative"; and community, "the city of God set on the hill of this world cannot be hidden." In regard to the silent life, "I see for myself the definite possibility of contemplative life in a community of men living in solitude and silence"; concerning possessions, "my call to poverty is simply a call to the cross….my treasure must be only in heaven so that my heart will be only in heaven."

John's prayerful thinking was to cover other topics, such as chastity, celibacy, obedience to vocation, stability, humility, music, and the Franciscan and monastic vows he knew he would take. Vague ideas began to take on concrete form in his mind, while concrete preconceptions were dispersed into clouds of mystery. As Chesterton wrote, "The one created thing which we cannot look at is the one thing in the light of which we look at everything. Like the sun at noonday, mysticism explains everything else by the blaze of its own victorious invisibility." John discovered that mystery in and of itself is a kind of revelation.

There were those who, upon hearing rumors about "the holy hermit in the forest," would travel long distances to seek out wisdom and counsel in John's cramped cloister. Some were priests, baring their doubts, questions, and even their souls in hours of penetrating conversation. Often John would learn as much as his visitors. He recalls, "They thought there was a holy man in the woods, but it was just me."

Here John underwent a kind of interior metamorphosis that would give direction to his journey and empower him to accomplish his tasks. He envisioned a prayer community in which many expressions would be lived out, from prayer to preaching, from the arts to manual labor, from receiving the Eucharist to living out the fundamental ideals of Saint Francis.

The vision, once seen in the darkness of his enclosure, seemed to expand with the brilliance and force of a sunburst. The possibilities seemed so endless, the promise so near at hand, the answer so profoundly simple. Just like Francis.

By January 1979, John had endured the dead of winter in a frozen cubicle with only his barely adequate bedding, chair, table, lamp and books. The chill of the air was hardly banished from the room by the primitive wood stove, which he stoked with dead trees and fallen branches. He had conquered the loneliness and severe conditions. He now felt ready to reemerge with new plans forged in the stillness of a hundred prayer-filled nights.

Using an old wood stove for heat, John spent the winter of 1978 in the little hermitage. It was from this solitude that he wrote the lyrics to *The Lord's Supper, Come to the Quiet,* and *The Painter.*

SCRC

Shortly after the release of The Lord's Supper I got a call from John Clauder from the Catholic Charismatic Renewal in southern California called SCRC, or Southern California Renewal Community. He had located me at my brother's apartment in LA. He wanted me to come sing at their convention at the Anaheim Convention Center. Coming out of the Jesus Movement, I was curious about these west coast Catholic Charismatics.

What I saw was a real education for me. Like the Jesus movement mega churches, I learned that there were many thousands of Charismatics in southern California. But what was different was their being a leaven in the dough of the parishes of the area, thus being almost invisible for most of the year. Only once a year they would gather together for a big convention. It was then that you could see how many, and how powerful a force they were, and are still today.

This became one of the best Catholic relationships of my ministry. I went down to Anaheim, hung out with the leaders, and did a concert in one of the larger rooms. It went very well. It was clear that some kind of extraordinary relationship in the Spirit was being birthed. Through the next 25 years I would join in their convention about every second or third year, doing concerts in the arena, and talks in their larger workshop rooms. I have always enjoyed participating in their life and vision.

Out of SCRC I made many good friends. The first was John Clauder, who was a drummer with the Mamas and the Papas. Next came the saintly Fr. Ralph Tichner, SJ, the founder and visionary of the Community, now deceased. Out of the many wonderful staff people, Dominic Berardino, Fr. Tichner's successor and the current president, became an especially dear friend.

> *Dominic is a true lay scholar, having one of the better private Catholic libraries I have ever seen. We still love to talk about our current studies in Church and monastic spirituality and history. He also has remarkable spiritual gifts in discernment and healing, as well as teaching and prophecy. He was first involved with the Kathryn Kuhlman ministry before coming back to the Church and getting involved in the Charismatic Renewal. Dominic is one of my great friends among the many I have made at SCRC over the years.*
>
> *~ JMT*

He planned a pilgrimage to the Holy Land in February—a fitting sequel to experiences at Alverna and in the hermitage. But before he left his hillside retreat, he recorded a growing conviction in his journal:

> "January 1, 1979, 9:00 PM. My heart longs for a reuniting of the people of the Christian faith...I believe the eschatological regathering of Israel, foretold by the prophets as a sign of the end times, symbolizes the regathering of the dispersed church back into her original homeland. I believe we will be substantially reunited before Jesus returns."

With this ideal in mind, John undertook an ambitious project—the writing of a volume entitled simply, *The Regathering.* The book was published in February 1981 in order to answer the deluge of letters inquiring about the thoughts of this "holy hermit". "In my opinion," John wrote in his introduction, "it is only in returning to this ordained, workable unity that Christianity will once more be a consistent, working manifestation of Jesus' simple truth and forgiving love. For where there is the truth of God's love, there must also be unity among God's people."[7]

A naive expectation? An impossible dream for the hopelessly divided body of Christ? Some would say so. However, the vehicle of reconciliation is often found where we least expect it. While synods, councils, and ecclesiastical task forces chaired by scholars and theologians hammer away at their meticulously worded documents from decade to decade, a gentle revolution of love and renewal was erupting around the world, bringing believers of diverse denominational persuasion face to face in fraternal unity. And on numerous occasions these winds blew the young troubadour into their midst to play his music and share his dreams of a grand family reunion of all Christian brothers and sisters.

One of the beauties of the Franciscan and monastic families is that, while it is strongly Catholic, it is also highly ecumenical in spirit and practice. There are participants from Protestant backgrounds, many of who are now forming their own monastic based prayer communities around the country. "I have tremendous hopes and dreams for those communities," John states with the enthusiasm of a carpenter at work for the Master Builder.

John began his work quietly, laboring in his own little portion of God's great church. Having just emerged from silent solitude, and bursting with an inner sense of purpose, he looked on in wonder as God unfolded a vast plan before him.

A Troubadour Sings
New Songs

As the date of John's departure for the Middle East approached, he made the decision to abandon his self-imposed imprisonment. He knew there would always be the call to solitude and that he would have to prayerfully balance active and contemplative pursuits. The hermitage experience was, in a sense, the inauguration of a cycle of action and meditation.

It seemed that God had taken this hillside tomb and turned it into a womb where the gift of music residing in John's soul was born and blessed with wings of flight. It would burst forth from the darkened cave with a force that would shortly be felt around the world. Indeed, this tour to the Holy Land was to be the first leg of an international itinerary that continues to this day.

Even before he reentered the outside world, it was apparent to all that *The Lord's Supper*, recorded before his retreat, was going to be a monumentally successful record album in Christian sales outlets. It is based on the Catholic Mass; although John had not yet converted at the time he wrote the music, he had been immersing himself in the liturgy as he prepared to enter the Church. The unbridled excitement at something about to be encountered, made this record energizing and charismatic.

"This was a surprise record," John recounts. "After going ahead with production I took the tape to Billy Ray Hearn for evaluation. At first Billy Ray said that he couldn't do anything with it. He humorously asked 'How are we going to sell a catholic mass to a bunch of Baptists?' When he played the record, things began to happen—people from down the hall at the Sparrow offices quickly appeared in Billy Ray's doorway wanting to know whose music it was. Some of them said it was the most beautiful music they had ever heard."

Billy Ray reluctantly signed the record into production on Birdwing, a division of Sparrow, undoubtedly wondering just how this Catholic-sounding product would be received in the predominantly Protestant book and record stores. It was a public relations and a business gamble.

"But the fact of the matter is, it just took off from day one," John adds. "The only thing I can say about that record is that it was a gift from God. It was not just me. It was the result of a community effort. I used a good orchestra, a good producer, and a group of brothers and sisters who sang spontaneously and worshipfully in what sounds very much like a charismatic choral session.

"When Billy Ray sensed the spirit of renewal that came through loud and clear on this album, he became excited about the potential for ministry to the broader Catholic market. He undoubtedly recognized it as the Gospel of Jesus Christ, which has no labels or boundaries," John says, feeling once again the exhilaration of those days when they knew they were onto something big.

But before John had a chance to be caught up in the attention his album had generated, he was off to the Holy Land. It would be a time of pilgrimage, and, for one who follows Jesus, a kind of homecoming. He walked the Via Dolorosa in Jerusalem, where the Son of God stumbled under the cruel weight of a

John's first trip to the Holy Land in 1979 would provide the inspiration for Light Eternal. John stands on the roof of Ecce Homo, over-looking the Temple Mount from the north.

Roman cross, and visited the holy places, including Christ's tomb, and the site of His birth in Bethlehem.

It was on this trip that his vocation in music began to come forth once again very powerfully but very naturally. In a letter written to Father Martin from Jerusalem, John conveyed his feelings:

> I have enjoyed Jerusalem, but it is the country-side that brings me really close to Jesus. The small villages are very much like those of Christ's time. I have enjoyed playing my guitar in the holy chapels and villages but I think the children of the villages have enjoyed it the most. The possibilities for a truly Franciscan apostolate as a troubadour for the Lord are quite exciting in a place where both the rich and poor reside within a stone's throw from one another.

The excursion was not without its more sobering moments, evident in the words John wrote toward the end of the same letter:

Never before have I seen such division and hatred. "Religion" is everywhere, but love seems so hard to find. The simplicity of the way of the cross is often forgotten, even though its geographical reminder is a part of daily life.

John visited priests, Franciscan hermits, monasteries, and many biblical sites, but the high points of his trip were Mount Tabor, the Mount of Beatitudes, and "just walking by the sea." In the changeless mountains and deserts of Palestine, John retraced the footsteps of his Master and his disciples while the call to his new lifestyle and ministry of music continued to take shape deep within.

One of the most important visits was with a Franciscan hermit and pilgrim named Fr. Arcadias. He was the spiritual father of Fr. Dacien Bluma, the Franciscan who had done so much scholarly work to revive Franciscan eremitism.

John met Fr. Arcadias at the Church of the Primacy on the north shore of the Sea of Galilee. Fr. Arcadias gave John permission to stay in his hermit's cave below Shepherd's Field outside of Bethlehem. John stayed in the cave by day, and slept in the empty friary at the holy site. The cave was primitive, but had a wooden front wall and door to keep out the elements. Inside was a table that served as a bed, and a primitive wooden cross. It was there that John learned a silent teaching by observing the natural contemplative life of the shepherds watching their flocks in the fields around the little cave.

Back home at Alverna, John wrote of these developments in his journal:

March 29, 1979, 2:00 PM. Since the recording of *The Lord's Supper*, my new direction in music has become a visible manifestation. My ideas concerning worship, art, entertainment, and liturgy have become reality. The trip to Israel caused me to reevaluate my entire vocation. Moving more into local ministry in the Franciscan community, in parishes and album projects is likely, plus continuing my contemplative life in a more organized fashion.

With all of this, I am truly amazed. It has all developed so quickly, and seemingly on its own. I have sought only the life of a solitary Franciscan hermit. I honestly thought that was the entire vocation for this part of my life. Then I find that just when I can begin to fulfill this contemplative call, God dumps all these other possible fulfillments of other calls right into the middle of my peaceful little hermitage. I have no choice but to follow the calls of God, if I am, in fact, professing the love of God. I continue to ask the prayers of Mary, Saint Francis, the angels, and all the saints both living and dead so that I might remain humble, simple, and obedient to love. In Jesus' name, Amen.

And well he might pray such prayers, for the hermit from Indiana was to find himself the object of increasing praise and attention from the record-buying public and the religious media. It seemed he was caught in a paradoxical bind. He sought quiet quarters and obscurity, away from lights, cameras, and crowds.

January 6, 1979

People have been coming to my cell door for two straight days. I cannot turn them away, for Jesus could not turn them away.   — From *Changes* by John Michael Talbot

The natural consequences of his call to recording, however, included increased popularity, inquiries by the press, and increasing demand for public appearances. It was with this conflict in mind that John wrote in his journal:

> April 25, 1979, 11:40 am. It is funny that in the time when success seems to be likely, my times of deep prayer keep calling me to a life of contemplative solitude. I cry with all my heart to be poor, and it appears I might be rich. I cry with all my heart to be despised and rejected, and it appears I will be accepted in love. I cry with all my heart to be humble and foolish, and it appears I might become a "wise man of God." All I seek is the death on the cross of Jesus, and it appears everyone is offering me only His resurrection. I am really frightened of my own frailty in this situation.
>
> It just all seems to be happening too soon. I don't feel at all worthy or ready. I don't feel I have ever really died, so how can I possibly be resurrected? I am still a novice in Jesus. I should still be taught; I should not be teaching! I am not worthy of a place of honor as a church liturgist. I should still be learning. I don't even read music well ... much less live a holy life!
>
> I pray that this is not all some deplorable temptation of the devil; He knows I would refuse blatant success or fame. But by disguising his scheme in piety, Catholic piety at that, he would make it hard for me, or anyone else, to discern. I must just submit to my spiritual adviser and believe that Jesus will guide me. God honors the humble and obedient.

In essence, John was offering himself advice that, as circumstances would soon demonstrate, was both timely and wise. Within a few short months of the day he wrote this journal entry, he was on the cover of *Contemporary Christian Music* Magazine and the subject of a feature article. The wall of seclusion that John had built to hold back the outside world crumbled. This was the beginning of a torrential flow of publicity that would find him written of, and interviewed in, newspapers and magazines (including *People Magazine, The Wall Street Journal,* and *The Saturday Evening Post*), and on national television.

Misquotes

Another thing that I have learned through the years is to keep spoken remarks to a minimum, because everything that I say can be misquoted by someone, and used against me. This cannot make us afraid to speak the Word of God, but it teaches us to do so with wisdom. As the scriptures themselves say, in many words there seldom lacks sin. ⁓ JMT

"Johnny has no concept of his fame," his mother said in the summer of 1980, as she sat in her sewing room making him a lightweight summer habit. I asked her why she thought this was the case. "Well, John is so intense, so deeply committed in what he does, that I just don't think he gives notoriety any real thought." John sat in the corner of the room sorting through some old photographs—he didn't appear to have heard a single word we said.

Fame

Fame is like a roller coaster ride. Anyone who has the talent and the perseverance to work their way up that first hill will have their moment on the top. That is not really the issue.

> *What really makes the difference is how long and how well they endure the ride after that first long drop. For some it is quite uneventful and short. For others it can be very interesting, and last a lifetime.* — JMT

This was a refreshing contrast to the inflated egos and flamboyant promotion of personalities found not only in secular show business but, sadly, among many Christian musicians. One sensed after having been around John that he was the genuine article—a true disciple of Christ who reluctantly accepted the spotlight as part of his task as a Franciscan troubadour. This kind of humility communicated more powerfully than promotional campaigns. It came from his marriage commitment to Christ, if you will, that the world began to see an enormous river of creativity surge forth, taking form as insightful lyrics, skillfully played tunes, and hundreds of pages of theological notes that would one day give rise to more books, articles, records, and performances. It was from this wellspring of inspiration that John drew forth his message to offer to a thirsty world.

Troubadour for the Lord book/Dan O'Neill

> *As the news of my Catholic conversion spread, it became clear that I would need to address the many questions that came from non-Catholic fans. I had met a lay Catholic theologian named Ed Durst who recommended that I speak with Dan O'Neill about writing a book.*
>
> *In 1980, Dan was a writer, and president of a new relief and development agency, Save the Refugee Fund, later to become Mercy Corps. He was about to become a Catholic, and like me, was looking for a vehicle to share the message of an evangelical plunging into the richness of the Roman Catholic faith. The project I proposed seemed a good opportunity for us both.*

> *Dan first came out to Alverna, and then to Eureka Springs before we moved onto the Hermitage property, interviewing me at length. I had never had to tell the whole tale, so Dan was most helpful in walking me through the process. The manuscript was enthusiastically accepted by Mike Leach, then president of Crossroad/Continuum, which was looking for a greater presence in the popular Christian book market. This project was ideal for them.*
>
> *The book soon became an award-winning best seller in the Christian/Catholic market, and was the start of friendships between Dan, Mike, and me that endure to this day. It would open into professional relationships between Crossroad and me in a successful writing career to augment my musical work. It would accomplish the same between Dan and me in a way that would flower into me becoming the honorary Chairperson of Mercy Corps. We have generated millions of dollars in aid for the poor through collections at my concerts. Dan and I would later collaborate on more book projects.*
>
> *Dan became a trusted friend and counselor to me personally, and to our newly forming community. Our relationship continues to grow as time goes by.* ∼ JMT

John recognized the benefits of the celibate life of ancient monasticism and Franciscanism, but he issued a word of caution. "Bonhoeffer warned that if you can't stand solitude, beware of community, and if you can't handle community, beware of solitude. I would carry that idea into human relationships by saying that if you can't handle celibacy, beware of marriage. If you can't deal with marriage, beware of celibacy. Celibacy cannot be a negative reaction against love relationships. It must be a positive embracing of a love covenant with Christ followed by a love for other brothers and sisters in the church."

There is also a certain loneliness in celibacy that creates an emotional pain from which one might become creative and expressive. To this John says, "Celibates who do not admit their loneliness are only fooling themselves. Celibates are often extremely lonely people. Their task, and the key to making their celibacy work for them, is in embracing loneliness and entering that dark night of the soul, coming into union with Christ, who cried out, "My God, my God, why has thou forsaken me?"

1980, during which John Michael released *Come to the Quiet*, *The Painter*, and *Beginnings*.

Come to the Quiet and For the Bride

After the success of The Lord's Supper, *I wanted to do something radically different. I wanted to record the Psalms I had been praying in the Hermitage at Alverna. I wanted a stark, yet spiritually rich recording.*

I played the demo tape to Billy Ray, who said that I had not sung with enough confidence, and that I had overcompensated with a performance that was too quiet. I then went into a little basement studio on the northeast side of Indianapolis, and recorded the basics in two days. Although the engineer was sick with the flu (you can actually hear him coughing on one of the tracks, despite the soundproof glass) the recording went very well, though it was not going in the direction of typical Contemporary Christian Music, which imitated secular music, except for the lyrics. The record company said this music had too much 'space' in it, and that the orchestrations sounded almost oriental in spots. They thought it was so bad that neither the producer (who is a friend to this day), nor the engineer wanted their names put on the cover of the album. Billy Ray said, "Well, you just had a big hit, so you can afford to lose $8000!" Little did any of us know that Come To The Quiet *would outsell* The Lord's Supper *and* The Painter.

For the Bride was also a departure from the standard CCM model. It was written as a ballet, and many Christian dance companies danced to it. This was a new phenomenon in Christian liturgical and worship scenarios.

~ JMT

John's subsequent albums for Sparrow/Birdwing expressed his experience of life at his monastery. Among others, they included an artful collaboration with Terry, *The Painter*, depicting Jesus as a master painter with his people as the canvas, *Begin-*

nings, which retraces John's musical development, *For the Bride*, communicating a delicate sense of musical ballet; *Troubadour of the Great King*, a double album with a theatrical quality commemorating the eight-hundredth anniversary of Saint Francis's birth, and *Light Eternal*, which could be characterized as high-church, neoclassical music.

John and Terry then reunited in the studio to create another album together, called *No Longer Strangers*. The title is taken from Ephesians 2:19. John has also recorded a series of albums with a distinctly liturgical style. Instrumental albums would later follow, and collaborations with old friends.

No Longer Strangers was a disappointment for John. To begin, the unique recording process of *The Painter* wasn't used. Sparrow wanted something more "down the middle." The vocal stacking was greatly reduced. It was also much cheaper to record. They added Abe Laboriel on bass and Keith Green's producer, Billy Maxwell on drums, but despite the virtuosity of the players, it just didn't work. Even the orchestrations of Lee Holdridge seemed to lack sparkle. But the songs themselves were much deeper lyrically. John feels that is the saving grace of the project. Despite this, Terry was so frustrated that he often left the sessions to go to the local gym to work out. John was left to work with Phil Perkins, Billy Ray, and the engineer, Ron Capone, who used to record Elvis. It worked, but it missed the mark of *The Painter.*

If a single thread of continuity is to be found running through John's numerous recordings, it is the spirit of renewal. The Greek and Hebrew words for breath also mean spirit. Through the rhythmic respiration of his singing, John has touched multitudes with the Spirit of God.

He describes his call in this poem:

> *To share the gift of music with all;*
> *For the rich and the poor,*

For the healthy and the sick,
For the young and the old,
For the strong and the weak;
To meet people where they are,
In the concert halls and on the streets,
In the churches and in the bars,
In the colleges and in the ghettos;
To never totally refuse an offer to sing because of money;
To never ask more money than what is offered;
To give the gift God gave in music as a gift to the world;
To give this gift back to God in songs of worship and praise;
To go forth as a troubadour for the Lord in the royal poverty of
Jesus, sharing the riches of this love in the songs I sing.

Little Portion
of the Ozarks

July 14, 1978

*Recently I have been burdened by the growing number
of young adults coming to me, of all people, for help. They
come from charismatic communities of both Protestant and
Catholic affiliations, yet are still unfulfilled in their search for
Christian community. They come from the '60s generation and
so are conditioned to looking for an alternative to the world in
which we live. Most see Jesus as the Source of this alternative,
but have yet to see a complete alternative in his Body. These
people want me to teach them for more than just one night.
They want to have me stay with them for long periods of time,
and some want to follow me. They come to me as their only
visible hope in the Body of Christ. I do not claim to be all
they say I am, but I feel I must help them if I can. Last night
I shared all of this with Father Martin. He agreed that something must be done.*

— From *Changes* by John Michael Talbot

The enormity of John Talbot's potential as a solo recording artist had become apparent by mid-1979. Many who had followed the Talbot brothers through their Mason Proffit days and their transition to Christian music were pleasantly surprised to see John's familiar face on a new album cover. A few were surprised, some even troubled, by his new look—short hair and a brown habit. Slowly word reached the industry and the public that John Michael Talbot had converted to Roman Catholicism and had become a Franciscan monk. True, there were a lot of questions, but judging from the sales of his albums, there was also a vote of confidence. Both Catholics and Protestants claimed him as their own.

Not only did he have a lot of recording work on his agenda, but also John had a fair amount of explaining to do in regard to his Catholic conversion. And, of course, there were his commitments to prayer, meditation, study, and writing, as well as his travel plans that threatened to overwhelm his simple lifestyle. Yet it didn't seem that any of these pressing plans could be dropped.

At this point, John's desire for community became more than a pleasant dream—it became an absolute necessity. And in a very real way he was already living in community at Alverna, where he continued to develop his philosophy about this way of life. "After all," John reminds us, "when two or three are gathered in Jesus' name, you have community; in this respect, all Christians touch upon certain foundational aspects of community."

In the beginning his dream for community flowed naturally from his life of prayer. The community was to be a support group of like-minded people, a base of operation that could facilitate the various functions of a multifaceted ministry. John decided to move ahead and formally establish a community of Third Order Franciscans dedicated to prayer, to preaching the Gospel, and to following the example of Saint Francis. But this was not an exercise in empire building, he determined; it would be a natural development. The focus would be on contemplative prayer rather than active ministry, so that both the life and the ministry of the community would be rooted in the power of Spirit-filled prayer. And so it began.

Troubadour of the Great King

After the success of The Lord's Supper, Come to the Quiet *and* The Painter, *I released a more highly developed work,* Troubadour of the Great King. *Terry and I had gone to England to overdub the orchestra on* The Painter, *and loved it. Our brotherhood grew in a new way as we tramped around London, me in my Army surplus blanket habit, and Terry in his hip, older brother look. We grew closer as we went to the places of great church and secular history. A love for London had taken hold of us both.*

Troubadour *was written in the House of Prayer at Alverna during the sweet Franciscan innocence and youth of our emerging community. When Phil Perkins came out to hear the songs, he expected the usual ten-song album, but something new was up. Instead of Phil choosing ten songs, he said that we had a double album set of material. He called Billy Ray, got the green light, and they went into the Barn Studios in Alexandria, Indiana.*

On this album, as is the case with most of my recordings, I recorded the guitar and vocals at the same time, to get a more live feel. Then we did some vocal stacking, like on The Painter *and* The Lord's Supper. *Then it was off to London.*

As the orchestrations were recorded it was clear that we had taken a major step forward in our musical maturity and quality. Phil's orchestrations were lush, and meshed beautifully with the more romantic and impressionist chord structures of the songs. We used a veteran classical engineer, Mike Ross, who

> *had started with all the rock bands of the sixties and seventies. He ran the studio like a ship's captain, and knew his room and his recording console inside and out. He was able to get wonderful orchestral sounds the likes of which we had never heard in the U.S.*
>
> *The orchestra was efficient, artistically excellent, and sounded great, using their best instruments in the recording session. They recorded fast, starting their rehearsal precisely at the top of the hour, something American players were not famous for in those days, and getting a take in just a few tries. We were told that great musicians don't need a lot of recording time to make great music. They were right.* ⁓ JMT

Just as Alverna had been the site of John's Catholic and Franciscan birth, it would also be the channel through which a new community would come forth, first called "Charity," then the Little Portion House of Prayer, named after the Portiuncula (meaning little portion) of St. Francis, and established by John under the supervision of Father Martin. With its handful of lay Franciscan brothers and sisters, the community took shape at the Alverna Retreat center. John began to pour himself and his earnings into this community over the next several years, in hopes of providing a model that could be replicated throughout the country as the winds of renewal produced more seekers.

John wrestled with the rule of his community, that is, how the lifestyle and the framework for authority and worship would take shape. The community would be primarily contemplative but also allow for active ministry, he determined. The community would incorporate flexibility in "Spirit-led living." It would also bring the call of the Friar and the Poor Clare into a working community of little brothers and sisters.

John sees the counterculture leaders of the sixties and early seventies as having asked many of the right questions concerning the bankruptcy of materialism, the problems of war and peace, the simplification of lifestyle, and the new directions in communal living. "The problem was that they didn't have Jesus at the center of it all, or a tradition on which to build," he says. "You could say they were doing the right thing for the wrong reasons, and now most of those experiments have died out. As Franciscans drawing on a wealth of history and models from church tradition, we had the building blocks to establish successful communities with Christ at the center."

"Some of what keeps people away from the idea of community," John explains, "is the simple fact that they define it too narrowly. Some think that community means cramped quarters, no privacy, excessive sharing, and submitting their own identities to some overriding, big brother type of legislation. The word 'community' doesn't necessarily have to mean proximity. It is much broader than that. It is a sharing of ideas and common values. In the case of Franciscans it is their desire to associate themselves in a way that acknowledges their common goal of following the example of Saint Francis. Benedictines, Carmelites, Augustinians and all other communities are similar in this way. Paradoxically," John concludes, "serious Christian community is both more simple and much more difficult than most people would expect. This is because it involves both the divine grace and the human responsibility of building relationships in God's love."

Often John would excitedly draw circles on restaurant napkins for friends and potential recruits: "We have several concentric circles of relationship moving outward from the center, which is God. First, we relate to Him. Then, of course, we have our families and close friends, followed by our church parish, and on out to the world. Many people need a level of support between family and parish, and that's the perfect level on which to establish communities that flower from the ministry of the Little Portion."

Light Eternal

Shortly after For the Bride, *I began work on a full classical project for choir and orchestra with Phil Perkins. It was the most ambitious work we had attempted,* Light Eternal. *Very few Christian or secular artists had mounted a project of this artistic distinction, and fewer still had tried it and been commercially successful.* Light Eternal *proved to be both.*

Phil and I worked jointly on the composition, and spent many hours at Phil's house developing the core work that I had written at the House of Prayer, then Phil added the choral score. We brought Lee Holdridge in to do the orchestrations and to conduct, because of his excellent work on The Painter, *and Billy Ray's* Hymns Triumphant. *The result was wonderful.*

One humorous situation occurred while recording the choral group in Los Angeles. We had written the work for two choirs, one a small ensemble, and another large choir. The small group was made up of Christian studio singers largely from the Lawrence Welk show. They were lots of fun to work with, being very reverent when singing a sacred piece, but also knowing how to have fun. One morning Phil and I came to the studio to find an already full parking lot outside, and the main studio lights off inside. As we came on into the control room the studio lights came on, revealing the entire group assembled around microphones, dressed in hooded bathrobes over their street clothes, with the hoods over their heads! They said that they wanted to make me feel at home in LA. It was hilarious.

— JMT

John's proposal would knit like-minded people together while bolstering the local parish with supportive activities. He repeatedly made the point that lay Franciscans need not wear a habit, sell all worldly belongings, or take restrictive vows. They may be married, students, business people, singles—they are only required to live according to the values of Saint Francis as far as they can within their personal circumstances.

"Also," John often said, "You don't necessarily have to be a Catholic to be a Franciscan in spirit. There are ecumenical Franciscans, friends of St. Francis, and Societies of St. Francis, in Protestant denominations." He outlined his thinking on this issue in a booklet entitled "Franciscan Community in Today's World."[1] In another work, "Secular Franciscan Houses of Prayer,"[2] John discussed the lifestyle specifics of his own community in a primitive Rule for day-to-day living. Many experienced religious voiced approval and wonder at where he got all of this. It was meant as an authentic compliment.

On a number of occasions I visited John at Alverna and we talked for hours about his dreams for the new community. The daily regimen was certainly more structured than a typical American's schedule. However, I found the budding Little Portion House of Prayer to be much freer than one might imagine a monastic setting to be. The day centered on the three to four offices[3]—these were hallowed moments spent together in a small chapel adorned only with the typical Franciscan crucifix of San Damiano.[4] Mornings were spent in quiet study or meditation, while the more active labors of the day were left for the afternoon. Meals were taken in common— kitchen duty was a rotating responsibility for all, including John, who claims to fix a "mean" grilled cheese sandwich and tuna casserole.

Depending upon their level of entry, position, and work in the community, members may or may not have worn the brown Franciscan habit. It is ironic that at a time when First Order Franciscans were abandoning their habits for street clothes, many new celibate orders of lay Franciscans and other spiritual families were putting them on.

"In wearing habits, we aren't implying that other communities like ours should wear them. We felt that for us they were significant," John stated. "By wearing my habit I am constantly reminded of my calling, and that I am God's property. It is a sign that the world seems to need and respect. It is a silent witness that speaks volumes."

It was not an uncommon sight to see John or one of the others stopping outside the kitchen door to feed or talk to "brother squirrel" or "brother rabbit," just like the Saint from Assisi and in his spirit—the spirit of the reconciliation of all things in Christ.

The Little Portion was a semi-eremitical community, in which solitary prayer and reflection held a central place, from which active ministry flows. The hermitage experience will always be available to members who may periodically retreat to seek God in quiet solitude and contemplation.

"The active work we did as Franciscans was, of course, very important," John allows, "but the real focus of our ministry was prayer, everything else was an outflow of the relationship we have with Christ in prayer. If we guard our prayer life, then we are guarding our ministry."

John's community mandate might seem introverted, but a closer look reveals a true concern for the entire world. "I believe we are moving into a prophetic time," he asserts. "We can no longer be passive about the call to unity, nor can we ignore the great issues of our day, such as poverty, injustice, and peace. I think that if we are in an environment that is attuned to God through prayer, we will be empowered effectively to address ourselves to these international concerns."

John soon forged an enduring relationship with Mercy Corps, a faith-based relief and development organization, based on his need to touch the world with compassion. He has raised many millions, and generated many more through matching grants for the poorest of the poor through Mercy Corps.

God of Life/Dana Scallon

Very soon after Troubadour of the Great King *was released, I began work on another project, keeping all of the things we liked from* Troubadour *while adding another dimension: Celtic music.*

I had been listening to Brendan's Voyage, *which combined Celtic instruments with a classical orchestra for a truly stunning outcome, and I immediately knew that I wanted to do a project incorporating Celtic music.*

At that time, I had also taken a real interest in Celtic monasticism. To me it was one of the greatest examples of the integration of states of life and spirituality in the ancient Church. I saw it as great model for a community like Little Portion, which integrated a celibate brotherhood, a celibate sisterhood, and families, as well as charismatic and contemplative spiritualities in one community. Double Celtic monasteries were not uncommon, and abbesses sometimes directed both men and women. It was an intriguing ancient form of monasticism to study as Little Portion built something rooted in the ancient, yet open to the new.

I had previously taken several ministry trips to Ireland, visiting the Carmelites outside of Dublin at a retreat house that had special gatherings of liturgical musicians. But this time, I went over with a friend, a Franciscan Friar named Fr. Ed, with whom I had done several photo shoots. Fr. Ed and I had arranged a trip through an Irish Franciscan Friar, who was to have arranged appearances all around the country. I was to perform in concert for the Catholic Charismatic Conference in Dublin at the RDS Coliseum, and then we were to visit local prayer groups and Secular Franciscan fraternities around the country, seeing much of Ireland in the process.

At the RDS Coliseum, I met a young lady named Dana and her husband. She was scheduled to sing before me. She had won the prestigious Eurovision Song Contest in 1970, and was quite well known in Ireland. She asked me for advice about singing in a Christian gathering. I gave her pointers about how singing for God was different than singing in the secular entertainment world, and that it wasn't just about entertainment. Some years later she would become very well known in the U.S. for writing the theme song for the World Youth Day 2000 in Denver. She would also enter politics and become Ireland's representative in the new European Parliament. She should have given pointers to me!

I will always remember the Irish crowd. After my performance, some enthusiastic concertgoers rushed the stage, and backed me against the rear of the stage, wanting autographs, prayers, or just to shake hands. I had never experienced anything like it in Christian music before, and was overwhelmed by their enthusiasm and faith.

After the high of the Dublin appearance, we went to the local Franciscan friary, named Broch House, or House of Bread. We were very warmly received, given a wonderful meal, and shown fine rooms. Then our host politely asked, "So why are you here?" We realized then that the Irish Franciscan who was to have set up the ministry itinerary had not made any arrangements at all. He had totally forgotten that we were coming!

The good Friars made hasty reservations for bus and rail passes for us to go anywhere we wanted to go. They quickly arranged for Fr. Ed and me to stay in their friaries, so we set out to see Ireland, and had a wonderful trip.

At each stop the Friars would welcome us warmly. We would join them for Vespers and supper, and then after some gathering where I would sing, we would congregate back in the recreation room of the friary. The friars would talk about Celtic Christianity and monasticism, or trade songs with me, until the wee hours of the morning. Then they would go to bed, grab about two or three hours sleep, and rise for Morning Prayer and Mass to do it all again! We couldn't keep up. But we got a great taste of Irish hospitality, music, and spirituality. The culmination of this Irish and Celtic experience was the God of Life project. I wrote the songs based on ancient Celtic prayers, using authentic Celtic instruments, like the Uilleann pipes, hurdy gurdy, Celtic harp, and Celtic drum. We integrated these instruments with the compositions, and then added a full orchestra. The result was a first for Christian music, and even for secular music at the time. It was only 1984, years before Celtic music and River Dance became fads in the United States.

I wanted to use a cover like the Book of Kells with the feel of a fully illuminated manuscript. A Franciscan sister did the artwork, and the result was truly stunning. But the company, thinking of the Christian Booksellers Association stores and customers, felt it looked "too weird" with the dragons and mythical creatures and such, and she was encouraged to "tame it down". It passed the conservative evangelical test, but it looked unimpressive compared to its original version. When the recording came out, people seemed to like it OK, but not many caught the full significance of the Celtic integration."

— JMT

In 1980, at Alverna, John felt directed by God to consider resettling the Little Portion community in Eureka Springs, Arkansas on John's acreage acquired at the zenith of Mason Proffit's fame and fortune. His instincts had been right. He had purchased the site of what would ten years later become the Little Portion Hermitage, and the Motherhouse of the Brothers and Sisters of Charity, the likes of which had never been seen anywhere in America. The ideas that came forth in prayer gradually took shape, and construction was begun on ninety-seven acres (now 450 acres) of Ozark Mountain land in 1982 with the support of Little Rock's then Bishop Andrew J. McDonald. It was a sobering venture that would involve zoning problems, design challenges, and hundreds of thousands of dollars. "Sometimes the idea of it scared me to death," John admits. "But it was a step of faith and obedience. It's incredible to see how God has provided everything—right down to an award-winning architect with an international reputation."

1980 – John Michael in an unguarded moment.

In the Ozark Mountains of Arkansas in 1982.

Architect Fay Jones, of E. Fay Jones and Associates had been recognized for his breathtaking design of Thorncrown Chapel in the woods outside of Eureka Springs, characterized by towering glass vaulting dramatically skyward in harmony with the trees that surround it.

"The vision I saw had little huts above ground, and most of the room for living underground. At first I wanted simple, inexpensive huts on the land," John said. "Then we found that we couldn't do that

Sparrow Records president Billy Ray Hearn (on right), and producer Phil Perkins join John for an inspection of the new property at Little Portion in the Arkansas Ozarks.

legally. So we determined to combine a number of concerns, including quality, simplicity, cost-effectiveness, energy efficiency, ecological harmony, and aesthetics. Fay came up with the perfect integration of all these requirements. The man is an architectural genius."

The property has a commanding view, sweeping some ten or twelve miles. Six pyramidal domiciles, hermit cells, or family residences were first built into the gently sloping hillside on the edge of a man-made lake, fitting in beautifully with the cedar trees. Each duplex-style dwelling housed two people. Also on the property were temporary buildings, a converted tool shed as a chapel, a common meeting area which included a library, a

The first chapel at Little Portion was a converted tool shed, shown here before the construction of the beautiful prayer garden.

kitchen, and a dining room, all in a $4,000 third-hand mobile home complete with a friendly gray snake who earned his keep by keeping the field mouse population down.

It was in the summer of 1982 that the Little Portion House of Prayer moved from Indianapolis to Eureka Springs. Before closing the final chapter of the Alverna experience, John sought the counsel of his friend and spiritual director.

"Father Martin," John ventured as they met together for a last time before the move, "I'm shaking in my boots. I don't want to do this—it's too big for me."

"Good," came the reply. "It's good to be afraid of what you are doing. Have a good healthy fear and know that you are just a small part of what God is really doing."

Little Portion's first common center was a $4,000 third-hand mobile home, which included a library, a kitchen, a dining room, and a friendly but elusive gray snake.

In the days leading up to the long overland drive John walked the grounds of Alverna with sadness in his heart. There was such mystery about the place, such enchantment. He could feel the years of Franciscan prayers bathing the forests and buildings. "You can feel it in the rocks, the trees, and the houses," John said wistfully. "And there is such love, such compassion, to be found there. It was the place where I was conceived as a Catholic—a place where I grew and was gently nurtured under the protection of holy friars, men of God. I was mothered, guided, and cared for.

"Before leaving I walked down to the creek and visited that hand-built hermitage where I had spent so much time in prayer. I cried, and I was scared. It was difficult—like a birthing process."

The Criterion, an Indianapolis newspaper, wrote a four-column story on John's departure under the headline, "Indianapolis to lose a man of prayer." John had become a fixture in the area and would be missed by many. He would have the pleasure of returning for major sacred music concerts, or "musical retreats," as many call them now, and would be received like a prodigal son.

Heart of the Shepherd

The Heart of the Shepherd *came after* God of Life, *and was our first use of purely digital recording. The lyrics, chordal expansions, and especially the arrangements by Phil Perkins came together in a way that became a trademark of my music—I wanted to bring the listener into God's simplicity without becoming simplistic or one-dimensional. These songs were very spacious in texture and tone. The album was one of the last to come out in the three still popular formats—vinyl, tape and CD.*

I went to record stores in Nashville and bought many classical recordings on CD to build up a digital collection. I spent many hours listening to classical and contemporary music in order to learn about the digital format. We also used one of the first digital studios in Nashville, owned by Norbert Putnam, a well-known studio session bassist turned producer who had worked with Joan Baez and Dan Fogelberg. From this experience we became more sensitive to quality performance, especially in the background vocal stacks, and in the new use of digital recording.

> *It is interesting that I still use many of the songs from* Come to the Quiet *and* Heart of the Shepherd *in concert. "Because You Are Chosen" and "St. Theresa's Prayer" were in that collection. The songs from that era continue to be requested, and remain a joy for me to pray in concert. It was right before the Reform of our community, and reflects some basic concepts, yet deep spirituality about Christian prayer and community life. People are still ministered to through those songs.* ∼ JMT

In those early years in Eureka Springs John and the core members of the community participated in the masses at Saint Elizabeth's and Saint Anne's in the neighboring towns of Eureka Springs and Berryville, often providing music and song in a supportive role. In an interview years ago, John said, "Each person in our community has special talents. Our outreach plans include radio production, music, drama, preaching, and dance. Like Francis, we will continue a street-level evangelism, using the arts to share the Gospel. We are particularly excited about developing artistic expressions for communicating the Gospel.

"There isn't any Bible-thumping or tract handouts—I've seen enough of that. And we aren't limited geographically," he added, referring to ongoing plans for tours to many cities to communicate their message of renewal, Franciscan and monastic spirituality, evangelism, worship, and charity.

"Funds are being raised to help people around the world, with a particular emphasis on hunger and refugee concerns," John said, his sense of social justice even more evident than in the seventies. At the height of the 1982 war in Lebanon he performed in a benefit concert, raising eight thousand dollars for Mercy Corps International. Mercy Corps provided desperately needed medical supplies during the siege of Beirut. For a time, John worked with Mercy Corps to establish a specifically Franciscan project called Franciscan Mercy Corps. As he developed this plan, he drew great strength and inspiration from Mother Teresa, whose work in India is known around the world.

With his extensive work with the poor through Mercy Corps, John began to resemble a musical version of Mother Theresa. He draws great inspiration from her, and considers her the St. Francis of our era.

John first met Mother Teresa at a conference in Fort Wayne, Indiana, on June 6, 1982, where they shared the stage and were featured in an article from which the following excerpted:

> Two special guests commanded the attention of the audience; John Michael Talbot and Mother Teresa of Calcutta…These two personalities were distinctive in their attire and attitude. Both conveyed an impression of simplicity and a mood of serenity. Contrasts and similarities were evident to those who knew them. One was garbed in brown, a Franciscan; the other dressed in white with blue borders, a Sister of Charity. One was from Indiana, the other from India. One was young, only 28, the other old, at 72. One was born in Oklahoma, the other in Macedonia. One grew up outside the church, the other within. One had a wayward childhood, reminiscent of Francis of Assisi; the other a consecrated youth, similar to Saint Clare of Spoleto. One calls himself the "Troubadour of the Great King," the other a "Mother to the poorest of the poor." One is named John, after the herald of Christ; the other is named Teresa, in honor of the patron saint of missions. Though this was their first meeting, John Michael Talbot, internationally known recording artist, and Mother Teresa, Nobel Prize winner, felt an instant kinship. Both have

taken with ultimate seriousness Christ's invitation to "seek first the kingdom of God, and his righteousness; and all these things shall be added unto you" (Matt. 6:33).[5]

Mother Teresa

I recall a humorous episode about Mother Teresa's ministry at that event. The speakers and special guests had been put up at a very large Crosier retreat house outside of Ft. Wayne Indiana. We would be shuttled to the event later that day. I thought that it would be good to prepare by some extra prayer, so I went down for Morning Prayer and Mass quite early. I entered the dark chapel, and found my way to a choir stall. As my eyes adjusted to the light, I saw Mother Teresa on the other side of the chapel. Of course, she was there before anyone else. But upon further observation I could see the head of this world famous, and most holy nun bobbing as she nodded off to sleep. I was reminded of Jesus sleeping in the boat with the disciples during the storm on the Sea of Galilee. I thought, "Well, if Mother Teresa could fall asleep in Choir, I guess I should not feel so bad for the times I have done the same!" Certainly, if anyone deserved to sleep in the mercy of God, it was she. She had just come in from an overseas flight from India. I would have been sleeping instead of trying to make Morning Prayer at all.

At that same conference I remember two things: First, was her scaring the Bishops to death as she proposed a decade of the rosary to the completely Ecumenical and Interfaith audience. Not one person seemed to mind! Second, I noticed that almost all of the sisters and nuns in the audience were in tears after hearing her simple words. She was not a great speaker, but the sincerity of her conviction stirred the reasons why most of these women had become brides of Christ and daughters of the

> *Church in the first place.*
> *For myself, I offered a recording of the Peace Prayer I had*
> *sung for her sisters. She complimented the setting of the prayer,*
> *but declined. She did not want her sisters to get used to the*
> *luxury of having tape players and radios. In those brief min-*
> *utes I felt that she was looking into my soul. Only one other*
> *person I have ever met has had the same effect on me: Pope*
> *John Paul II. Certainly these are two of the saints of our era.*
> — JMT

This illustrates again the paradoxical path on which John finds himself. One day he is, in a manner of speaking, hiding in hermitage, far from prying eyes and enveloped in solitude and quiet, while the next day he may be singing in a peace march at the United Nations or appearing with a noted personality at a public function. It follows the pattern of Francis, who found himself alternately in the presence of the Pope and pauper.

But John also feels a special kindred relationship to Saint Bonaventure, a Franciscan reformer of great intellect who brought balance to the movement when it was threatened with excesses in certain areas. Bonaventure symbolizes a greater integration of the monastic wisdom of the past into the Franciscanism of his own day. There is a necessary tension between the freedom of Francis and the organization of Bonaventure that John will need to maintain a disciplined equanimity if, indeed, he is to establish similar communities as part of his ongoing work. This awareness brought John into a deeper desire to study the roots, not only of the Franciscan movement, but also of the older monastic forces that helped shape Francis's own vocation and the Franciscan communities. He saw the study and application of church history as indispensable to the mission to which he is called.

Songs for Worship

Before and after God of Life, *I decided to use some more settings of liturgical texts. I had experienced the dread of having to sing poorly written Catholic music composed since Vatican II, yet I knew that in order to get the musical 'wheat', I would have to allow for ten times as much 'chaff'.*

I had been composing liturgical settings since I had become a Catholic, but had never put them together in a thematic work, except for the more choral Masses. These texts were primarily Psalms, and some more Masses that were less choral, which were better suited to the guitars used most commonly throughout the churches in America.

I had actually started the compositions as a capella pieces for a small vocal group, but this soon changed as I realized the limitations of such pieces, both in terms of performers and listeners. So I ended up recording them with what had by now become a more standard sound for me. Only later, on Cave of the Heart, *would I finally take the a capella approach with some motets.*

The first Songs for Worship *album was fairly standard in it's recording, and in its reception from listeners. I think that the second collection is more interesting. It began as another ambitious project of assembling a small group of singers at Little Portion Hermitage, and putting together an accompaniment recording to a larger songbook, made up of 150 liturgically oriented Psalms, songs, hymns, and masses. About half of these were my compositions.*

The Songbook did well, but we learned early on that we could not compete with the larger liturgical companies such as Oregon Catholic Press, GIA and NALR. It was actually very simple, for due to their size, they heavily influenced the music that was played in the parishes of America, and understandably wanted to promote their own collections and copy-

> *righted songs. This left us at a huge, and almost insurmountable disadvantage in the area of liturgical music. Yet the songbook still did well, though not nearly what we had hoped for. I was very pleased with Songs for Worship II, taken from the larger songbook. The chorus, the songs, and the orchestral treatments all came together nicely. It is a project I have always favored from that liturgical period. But we learned that my music could not be primarily liturgical, but was simply sacred music with only occasional liturgical applications.* ⁓ JMT

"As we look more deeply into our past, we find patterns of renewal that, contrary to being archaic voices from the past, prove to be excitingly relevant to the issue presently facing us," John explains. A 1982 trip to Ireland greatly helped John to determine some of the forces that influenced Franciscan tradition and ministry.

"I know I'll never get to the end of discovery when it comes to the study of monasticism, history, and their relationship to our own call, but what I have learned is both helpful and incredibly interesting," John reports. "I found that in the tenth, eleventh, and twelfth centuries Irish Celtic monks passed through Italy on pilgrimages to the Holy Land, and evidently had great impact on the religious environment into which Francis was born. It was under the influence both of the Eastern desert fathers and of the pilgrim monks from the north that Francis developed a new integration of mystical prayer and Gospel poverty, allowing the friars to be both itinerant wandering preachers as well as contemplatives. This, of course, led to a major renewal of faith in the thirteenth and fourteenth centuries." John speaks with the assurance of a scholar, leafing through volumes of notes and reference material as he talks.

He went on to explain that Franciscan missionaries had reached Ireland by 1228, a mere two years after the death of

Francis of Assisi. Since that time, Franciscans have had a major impact on the people of Ireland. Remaining true to their original vision of prayer and poverty, the friars and sisters were considered holy men and women of prayer, and they were always accessible to the poor. It is easy to understand why Franciscans have always been greatly loved by the Irish.

It is of interest to note that the Franciscans also reached China shortly after the death of Francis. Donning the robes of the Confucian and Taoist sages, they preached and lived the gospel of Jesus in a way the Chinese could understand. The Jesuits did the same with great success as well, and there is some evidence of a similar approach by Syrian Christian monks as early as the 7th and 8th centuries. All of this points with radical significance to interfaith dialogue today, and its effects on mutual cooperation and respect between the world's great religions. It also exemplifies a humble and respectful evangelism that uses the good and wholesome religious expressions of the people to whom we present the gospel of Jesus, as the complement and completion of all good that has come before.

John put this same winning combination into effect at the Eureka Springs community and elsewhere. From the beer-drinking friars of Dublin to the tee totaling Baptists of the American South, from the high liturgy of Roman Catholic Mass to the Pentecostal prayer service of the Protestant community churches, John sees a faith unified in its central theological points and people whose hearts are set to serve the Lord in spite of cultural and traditional diversity.

"Saint Francis bridged all those gaps in his own lifetime, and so did those who followed in his humble footsteps. In a truly Christian, truly loving community, different personalities blend to create a more complete picture of Jesus," explains John. "And after all, he is the one we want to show to the entire world. This is our challenge."

Monks and Monasteries

A monk is a person who seeks God alone. A monk is a person on fire with love for God, one who has given up all and separated himself from all in order to know intense mystical union with the Creator of all. A monk should be like a man from another world. The things of this world should be totally tasteless to him. Yet in this holy detachment, the monk should be the person who comes truly to experience the created world with a heightened awareness and heavenly appreciation that comes from knowing the Creator of the world. The monk is the one who turns only to heavenly realms, and so becomes effective on earth. The monk seeks to be a divine creature from another world, and so comes to bring the human reconciliation of Jesus to this world. The monk seeks to be a pilgrim and a stranger, and so is everywhere at home.

Likewise, the monastery should be like a dwelling from another world. The allurements of the secular city should be totally absent in this city of God. Yet the monastery should be a place of true artistic beauty and environmental balance, reflecting as a mirror on the earth the heavenly beauty and balance of the divine Artist. The monastery should be a place of keen environmental beauty and sensitivity, where the delicate and fragile dimensions of all creation are fully experienced, appreciated, and savored, so as to lead the solitary community of monks to constant praise of God. Let the monastery be a place of silence, so that both the small and the great dynamic reality of the Living Word of God will always be sensitively received. Let it be a place of environmental asceticism, so as to foster a heightened awareness of the delicate aesthetic beauties of the created world. Yes, let the monastery be like a dwelling from another world, and it will increase sensitivity to the created beauty of all the world and so help lead all creation to God. ⌐ From *Hermitage* by John Michael Talbot

A Hermitage cell at Little Portion Hermitage today.

A hermitage in
the Brothers'
Grove.

The sisters' skete was completed in
February of 1990.

Aerial view of
Little Portion
today.

Reform, Renewal
and Change

The Little Portion Hermitage monastery dream material-
ized marvelously by the end of 1983 when initial construction
and landscaping were complete. It was a beautiful slice of natural, Ozark beauty with structures reflecting simple yet dramatic
design.

The small group of followers that joined John Michael on
this new phase of his pilgrimage deeper into monastic life
desired to share in community, to be radically committed in
their faith, to be loyal to their church, and to avoid the pitfalls of
fundamentalism. Among early community members were five
or six who had taken private vows in the Secular Franciscan
Order (SFO). It was a time of experimentation, forging new
frontiers, coalescing around shared values—a time of trying and
testing.

A social scientist once said that a certain, predictable devel-
opmental sequence emerges in any long-term group process. In
partnerships, marriages, businesses, or communities, four phases
will become evident if the group process is managed success-
fully: forming; storming; norming; performing. The group *forms*
for the purpose of realizing a shared goal or a vision. *Storms*

emerge as the inevitable conflict enters into the relationship dynamic. *Norming* is the appropriate application of conflict resolution skills. Finally, *performing* is the realization of the initial objective in establishing the group. Frequently, in partnerships or social groups, there is great surprise at the emergence of conflict. And it is in the conflict mode where disillusionment can enter, where cracks form in relationships, and where disintegration takes place unless renewal can somehow be achieved.

By the mid '80s a few storm clouds began to appear over The Little Portion community.

"It seemed like we were trying everything and achieving next to nothing, except with my music and books," John recalls. "We were becoming bogged down, some even began to 'fry' emotionally, because we were trying to do so much with so few people who were, at best, novices in this way of life. We were democratic to a fault – we even voted on what dog food to buy! There was no clear direction. Some wanted a more intense expression of religious life. Some wanted less discipline, and yet more freedom to go into town, or out to dinner, or to a movie even more frequently. Some sisters wanted a veil, and others did not. Likewise, there were differences of opinion among the brothers concerning the habit. Dissent began to erode the ranks of our already tiny community. We called ourselves a 'hermitage,' but in reality most of our members were living pretty undisciplined lives. St. Francis called such hermitages 'cesspools of pleasure'. I used a very passive form of leadership, and hesitated to take proper authority as founder. Frankly, I was still very new to this way of life and simply didn't know how to lead yet." The ship of community had started to drift.

The beginning of the Rule of St. Benedict describes the four types of monks. Those who live in community under an abbot are cenobites. Those who live in solitude after first being tested as cenobites are hermits. The other two are negative, sarabites and gyrovagues, and include those who gather informally in small groups without clear leadership and obedience. We were coming dangerously close to this traditionally destructive form of quasi-monasticism.

This 1984 photo taken at Graymoor, New York, was from the photo shoot for the book *Changes*.

Jamie Talbot, who had by now moved to take up residence and, ultimately, permanent vows at the community, observed her son's unrest with concern. Late one afternoon as John shared his heart with her, his frustration rose and he posed the unthinkable:"Mom, maybe I should just leave…"

Jamie paused for a long moment and then quietly responded, "Johnny, you are the founder of this community. You have invested your life and your resources in this place. You just tell them your vision and they can decide if they want to be part of it!"

John prayerfully and quietly pondered these words in his heart. What is the vision? Who shall be numbered among us? How should we live in community? In 1986 John took a brief leave from the community to visit trusted friends in Seattle and Nashville. He dared to ask himself the most fundamental of questions: should I enter the priesthood? Should I consider married life? Do I really want to lead and manage a religious community? Long-time, close friends, including Fr. Martin, provided solace, support and space to think quietly.

Fire of God/Meditations on the Gospels

About this time I began to work on another book, The Fire of God *that went beyond the biographical* Troubadour for The Lord, Changes, *and* The Lover and the Beloved. *Our community had grown so "contemplative" that it was starting to get lazy, and I wanted to fire up some enthusiasm in the Spirit—my writings of that period clearly reflect this.*

The Fire of God *divides spiritual life in Christ into three categories: starting a fire from kindling, building up a roaring flame, and developing hot coals. The kindling is the seemingly artificial means of an ascetic, or abstinent discipline. The roaring fire is the enthusiasm of the Holy Spirit. The steady hot coals are the resulting, more contemplative life. Each is needed in its own time, and helps build and prepare for the other. Kindling prepares the fire, but will not burn long on its own. The Roaring Flame builds obvious, visible fire, but will actually draw heat out of a house, and burn out if left to burn too long. After the Roaring Flame, Hot Coals are left through the natural burning process. The Hot Coals are what heats the house of the soul for the long term, but cannot be built without the others, and are not nearly as flamboyant or impressive. If the coals are hot enough, they will burn until the next morning, and can be used to get the Kindling started again. With this analogy it aggressively treats various social issues such as global poverty, pro life, ecology and weapons of mass destruction.*

After this I began work on the three-volume Mediations on the Gospels, *which takes the reader through the liturgical year. These books were assembled using the content of my morning talks to the community during the Communion service, and were especially focused on a more radical approach to hearing and living the Gospel. It was very charismatic, but was based on solid monastic and Franciscan spirituality. Jack Hayford called the series, "raw Spirit power."*

After that, I completed a book on the Beatitudes, Blessings. *This book puts the culmination of my spirituality at that time into the context of the Beatitudes. But in some ways I was disappointed, because I didn't really come up with the title. It was the publisher's idea. In many ways that book is begging to be rewritten with a maturity that comes from many more years. Maybe someday I'll get to that.*   ⁓ JMT

And then a new thing happened. Blowing into the community like a fresh, spring breeze came Sr. Viola Pratka, an Incarnate Word nun from Victoria, Texas. She was introduced to the community while helping to sponsor a concert with the Dallas Symphony Orchestra. She didn't really like John Michael all that much, and thought his introversion was conceit. But she liked what she heard about the community. Intending to take a sabbatical at the monastery, she provided new eyes and a seasoned faith perspective on life at Little Portion Hermitage. With 25 successful years of religious life and training to her credit, Sr. Viola plunged into fervent prayer and joyful labor, all the while sizing up this new community. She found problems but also found great promise. When John Michael returned to the monastery after his brief time away, he found himself engaging in deep conversations and many hours of prayer with this nun from Texas, 14 years his senior. Some community members were not happy with her more disciplined and enthusiastic input from her experience in consecrated life and wanted her to leave. But she was bringing this much-needed experience to the community from the inside out, not just from the outside in.

John asked Sr. Viola to take an increasing leadership role in the community and, with Fr. Martin, even suggested she consider leading the sisters of the monastery. This would involve a formal dispensation of her vows from Rome, and a transfer to the Brothers and Sisters of Charity. Out of humility and fear, she refused two times, but the third time was a charm. She humbly accepted the encouragement of John Michael and Fr. Martin. She began simply, but with clear vision of one experienced in religious life and discipline. She suggested cycles of work and prayer with Wednesday and Friday fasts to provide more monastic rhythm to community life. Additionally, she assessed community expenses and managed to provide meals for less than 50 cents per meal, thereby saving funds and establishing a new level of simplicity. Clearly, Sr. Viola Pratka was bringing new life and new hope to the brothers and sisters around her.

One of the things that changed was a shift from a lack of discipline in the name of eremitism, to a more disciplined cenobitical, or communal life together. "In this we discovered that during those morning hours for prayer, many were piddling their time away, or just sleeping, or worse," John says. "People new to consecrated life rarely have the self-discipline to use their 'free' time for intense work, study, and prayer. It takes years to develop. That is why the traditional model where the eremitical life is still lived is to spend ten years or so in the cenobitical life before moving into hermitage." John continues, "So the community shifted a bit more towards the cenobitical model, and had all new members put in a good day's work, and report regularly on their daily schedule and spiritual progress to a leader."

John sensed a new spark in his spirit for the potential this developing religious community could have. He prayed, studied and examined religious communities from wide historical and geographic perspectives, investigating their canonical status and possibilities for adaptation. He studied the development of the Rules and Constitutions of Cistercians, Carmelites, Camaldolese, Carthusians, Benedictines and Franciscans. He had struggled with drafting his own Rule and Constitution for over a year until Sr. Viola offered a suggestion. "John, just write from the scriptures!"

Catholic communities have different documents to reflect, guide, and legislate their life. A "Rule" like the Rule of Benedict, the Rule of St. Francis, Augustine, or the Carmelites was the primitive core document for communities up to the 13th century. The "Constitution" is the core document for communities today, and either further describes the ancient communities of the spiritual family's founder before the 13th century, or is the sole core document for later communities. The "Statutes" or "Directories" are more detailed concerning consecrated life in a community at a particular time or place. Lastly, similar to a secular business, there are policies and procedures. Church authority through the diocesan bishop or the pope must approve the core documents.

By the mid–sixties, the school principal was scandalized by the length of John and Terry's hair. This promotional photo shows the new look and direction of Sounds Unlimited.

October 1969, at the beginning of Mason Proffit.

1968 – The beginning of the Mason Proffit look. Terry below, and John on the right.

In 1971, five months before his eighteenth birthday, John and Nancy were married in an Indianapolis Methodist church.

Alverna Retreat Center in Indianapolis in 1977.

"I spent most of the time on my knees, crying before the Lord," recalls John, "or wandering around the grounds playing my guitar."

At Alverna in 1979, with Amy. John was writing
"Peter's Canticle" for *Come to the Quiet*.

August 1978 – John begins to build his hermitage in the woods
at Alverna. The curved rock wall is the back of the Shrine to
Our Lady of Lourdes, and served as one of the interior walls
of the hermitage.

December 1978 – John's hand-built hermitage in the woods. "I remember that birds would land on my shoulders when I sat in meditation outside. The things of Francis are more than quaint stories. They can be true if we dare to try ourselves."

"I remember the little mouse that used to come in through the front door of my hermitage. I fed him cheese and breadcrumbs. He would stand on his hind legs and beg, just like a dog."

John Michael in 1980, overlooking St. Elizabeth Catholic Church in Eureka Springs.

In 1980, John and Terry met at their mother's apartment in Indianapolis, and worked on a song for Terry's third solo album.

1980 – On the cover of *New Sound*, a Boston-based Contemporary Christian Music promoter.

February 17, 1989 – John Michael and Viola marry at Charity Chapel at Little Portion Hermitage. Bishop Andrew J. McDonald of Little Rock officiates, assisted by Deacon Sam Hillburn, left, and Fr. Martin Wolter, right.

At the mission at San Juan Capistrano, California, in 1989, shortly after his marriage to Viola.

In the Holy Land at the Mount of the Beatitudes
with his mother, Jamie.

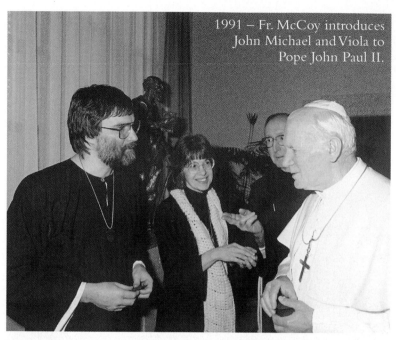

1991 – Fr. McCoy introduces John Michael and Viola to Pope John Paul II.

February, 1983 – John Michael lends the construction crew a hand as concrete is poured into wall forms for a new hermitage.

John Michael and Viola at the groundbreaking ceremony for the sisters' quarters, also known as a skete.

Community members take a break and enjoy a picnic on the grounds of Little Portion Hermitage Monastery.

John and Viola enjoy a picnic outside of his mom's hermitage at Little Portion in 1996.

A view of the Little Portion Retreat and Training Center at More Mountain in Eureka Springs.

A brother calls the community to prayer from Little Portion's bell tower.

Visitors first see the view of the bell tower and front of the Common Center at Little Portion when they arrive.

In 1999, this photo was used for
Cave of the Heart promotion.

Brothers and Sisters of Charity, Domestic, assist Viola at a concert
and teaching in California in 2001.

John performs in concert at the Southern California Renewal Community's annual convention in Anaheim in 2001.

The new Portiuncula chapel at Little Portion built in 2002.

John Michael shares the concept of seated and walking meditation at a stop during a prayer walk at Mission San Juan Capistrano in 2000.

Bishop Friends

There are two bishops that have had a most positive effect on my life and ministry. The first is Andrew J. McDonald, Bishop Emeritus of Little Rock. He welcomed me to the Diocese of Little Rock in 1982 before we began construction of the Hermitage. He always signed his letters, "Your Friend," and there is no doubt that he proved to be such in Christ and the Church over and over again. When we first came to Arkansas, Bishop Andrew preached reasonably well as a bishop, but it was in the typical style of political correctness necessary for those who fill this role in the Church. But in later years he became more daring in his preaching style, without losing his balance. He became an authentic evangelist and prophet. It was like he had been set on fire with a fresh empowerment of the Holy Spirit. He began to preach as if the life of our whole society depended upon it, and indeed it still does. Yet that evangelistic fire was tempered by a great wisdom that only the experience of 25 years as bishop could bring.

Bishop McDonald was truly the Episcopal father to the Brothers and Sisters of Charity, and he will always hold a singular place in the heart of the community, and in the hearts of all who personally remember him. When he retired there were many in the diocese who wept tears of gratitude and fondness for having been granted such a true friend in Christ for a bishop for 25 years. Today, Bishop J. Peter Sartain has succeeded Bishop Andrew, and the relationship follows in this same tradition of spiritual friendship, great preaching, and great wisdom in Christ and the Church.

I first met Archbishop Bernard Cardinal Law when he was bishop of our diocesan friends to the immediate north, in Springfield/Cape Girardeau, Missouri. I had been invited to give my testimony in the Cathedral with Dan and Cherry O'Neill in a live taping for the new Catholic TV network launched by Mother Angelica. At that time he graciously invited me to stay in his house anytime I flew out of Springfield on ministry (It is one of the closer airports I used for fly out ministries). I took him up on it on several occasions. There was no telling whom you might meet there. I remember not only diocesan leaders, but also Fr. Mike Scanlon and Ralph Martin, among others, who found a good friend in Bishop Bernard Law. On those occasions it would not be unusual to "raid the icebox" in the kitchen, and warm up a snack after several hours of dialogue about God, Jesus, and the Church. Bishop Law always seemed to intuitively understand exactly what those of renewal and reform in the Church were trying to do, and he was always willing to lend appropriate support.

During those times sometimes just the two of us would celebrate Mass in the bishop's private chapel in his residence. I have had the opportunity to do this on occasion with many priests, diocesan and religious, and even some bishops. But I have never experienced such an intuition of the presence of the entire Church universal as during these times with Bernard Law. The man's awareness of the Church is palpable, and gives him greatness as a Bishop.

I also knew that he was a man quick to respond to the more charismatic gifts at work in him through his being a bishop and successor to the apostles. During the blessing of our Hermitage on October 4, 1983, to which he was invited as bishop of an adjoining diocese, I felt a tap on my back. It was Bishop Law. God had inspired him with a scripture, so he asked to share it. He read it with great power, and shared his thoughts impromptu. All in attendance were greatly moved.

At one point Fr. Martin suggested that I get someone geographically closer to act as my spiritual director. He had been assigned up in Indiana with the Friars to help with the novitiate, and felt that someone closer would be more available. After much prayer and dialogue Bishop Law agreed to be my spiritual director. We had not proceeded very far into that more formal relationship when the Bishop received word of the possibility of a new assignment in Boston or New York. It would be a major change either way. I prayed that it would not be New York. I was afraid that such a place of global prominence would change him. As it turned out, another Bishop who had brought me into Pennsylvania was appointed to New York, the late Cardinal O'Connor. Bishop Law was sent to Boston. He would inevitably become a Prince of the Church as one of the few Cardinals in America.

This was brought home graphically to me when, on the way into Boston to sing at his first Mass with the religious brothers and sisters of the Diocese, we pulled into a tollbooth at the edge of the city, and asked for the quickest route to the Cathedral. It looked like we were going to be a little late. The Boston Police immediately gave us an escort to the Cathedral, with their sirens blaring and lights flashing. I knew that we were "not in Kansas anymore!"

After he was installed as Archbishop of Boston, and subsequently named a Cardinal, I would still visit in the much more imposing Cardinal's Residence near St. John's Seminary. Though the level of leadership was unquestionably higher, and more influential for the Church in America, Bernard Law remained interiorly pretty much as before. We would still stay engrossed in dialogue about the things of God, and "raid the icebox" after the sisters who took care of the residence were long gone. Beneath all the inevitable pomp and ceremony that accompanied the higher level of his new assignment, he was still the same Bernard Law at heart. He was still a humble servant of God. It was reassuring to see such power remain something extrinsic to his life in Christ. — JMT

Eventually, a Scripture Rule was drafted which gave new life, focus and vision to The Little Portion Hermitage. The Constitution and Directories would come soon after. Three themes began to repeatedly occur to John Michael in his mornings of contemplative prayer. "Die to Franciscanism. Don't put new wine into old wineskins. Build community by not building community." These were startling contradictions, or at best paradoxes, to be sure, and would seem to have laid an ax at the very root to the still budding religious community. However, these ideas would ultimately give The Little Portion Hermitage a unique angle on such communities in North America. When John combined these thoughts with the ancient, Celtic, integrated monastic model, which included not just celibates, but singles and families, the possibilities, became truly exciting. And motivating.

He saw how the 11th century reforms of Benedictine life had increased their monastic discipline, while at the same time opening the life up to as many states of life as possible. The Carthusians, Camaldolese, and the Cistercians, just to name three, integrated priests, lay brothers, and conversi or domestic brothers who, for whatever reason, could not profess the vows, and live the life as intensely as the other monks. They also included lay oblates that lived in the villages and farms around the monastery. From this he saw an ancient model for the integrations needed today.

He began to see all monastic and consecrated life from the Christian East and West, the simple living tradition from the "plain people" from the Anabaptist and Utopian early American heritage, and even interfaith monastic expressions, as ancient sources for modern monastic living rooted and centered in Christ. It was as if a Divine light had some how been turned from the "off" to the "on" position in his heart and mind, spirit, soul, and body.

"I also began to think of our community's reform in terms

of the example of the Vatican II experience—there was the
clear reform of the structure of the Church that was followed by
the wind of the Spirit, not unlike Ezekiel's 'dry bones' prophecy.
First came structure, then the flesh, followed by renewal in the
Spirit. Suddenly, it all made sense. We began to navigate a new
course with the wind of the Spirit at our backs!" John exclaims
today. "Of course, we didn't find perfection. We simply found
our way."

Those community members who did not fully support the
reform process were offered time away to prayerfully reflect in
order to make more informed decisions. Several took the offer.
Some would never return. New inquirers and postulants continued to arrive, many from cities in which John Michael Talbot
had performed concerts. Some came from countries half a globe
away.

As the new Rule and Constitution developed and as community policies and procedures were established, a framework
was created whereby renewal could be ignited and sustained.

A match was about to be struck.

In the prior years a group of lay people became associated
with the new community. They were called "Associates," but
were about to become something more.

As community members and associates converged upon the
Alverna Retreat Center in Indianapolis for a conference, an
amazing outpouring of the Holy Spirit seized the group following Mass. There were expressions of unrestrained joy, worship and praise followed by prayers in which people would fall
as though "resting in the Spirit". A sense of renewal began to
sweep through the group and continued with ever-greater
numbers of associates and friends looking into membership in
the community. The flames of renewal were fanned throughout
the country and, indeed, new wine was poured into new wineskins as the associates became authentic members of the
monastery, but lived in homes across America, becoming offi-

cially recognized as Brothers and Sisters of Charity, Domestic. A dramatic "Eureka Springs Thanksgiving Experience," as it has come to be known, followed the "Alverna experience". Following a wondrous Thanksgiving Day celebration at the monastery, community members in various groups went for outdoor walks. Some began to see the sun "spinning" as had been widely reported in the miracles of Medjugorje. Sr. Viola began to notice the color of the landscape shifting to a golden hue. "Believe it or not, I am usually quite skeptical about such phenomenon on a daily level, but it was very clear something amazing was happening," John Michael recounts. "It was as if gold light were being projected from the heavens and was glowing out of objects. We literally observed golden crosses of light on the dirt road. Later, stones the shapes of hearts were found everywhere, and still are today. Many, including my mother (also skeptical of such things), noticed that the lake was sparkling and multi-colored—this lasted between one and two hours."

These experiences seemed outrageous to some, and miraculous to others. One thing is certain, for the newly reformed community these events acquired a dynamic like the outpouring of the Spirit at Pentecost for the first followers of Jesus. The community was founded on principles of integration, including the charismatic and contemplative spiritualities. It had emphasized the contemplative life to the point of neglecting more enthusiastic and charismatic forms of worship. It was time to balance things out, so God set the new movement on fire.

It seemed a miraculous confirmation of the renewal that was clearly upon them. These events were reported to Bishop McDonald of the Little Rock Diocese. He was cautiously open and began regular visits to the community. There was a palpable enthusiasm for Jesus, the Church and community throughout the membership of The Little Portion Hermitage among both monastic members and domestic. Electricity was in the air.

Regathering and Hiding Place

The Regathering *was a full-blown contemporary orchestral and choral album, reflecting the far-reaching ecclesiology and theology of the regathering God had put on my heart with love for the Evangelical and Catholic gatherings of believers. It was a call to the unity of Regathering from the scattering of the New Testament Protestant Diaspora that shook the lethargic Catholic Church. The call was nothing less than a self-critical call to radical gospel living according to the teaching and examples of the Church and her saints. Yet it also called Evangelicals to recognize the gifts found in the Catholic faith. It was a sword that cut, and continues to cut, both ways. A book, also titled* The Regathering *was also released.*

The troubles associated with the Reform of the community were starting to weigh heavily on me at the time, and all had not gone well with some who left. I had been slandered, gossiped and lied about despite my repeated attempts at reconciliation. Some called it down right character assassination. I had sought counsel and solace from the Church in the person of the Bishop, who wisely counseled me through the stormy waters of reform and public opinion. It was here, through this brokenness, that I experienced a whole new way of embracing the cross.

The music and the liner notes of Hiding Place *reflect my spirit at the time—on the heels of* The Regathering, *Billy Ray asked me to do something simpler, without becoming simplistic. I reached deep into that brokenness for the right Psalms, scriptures, and melodies to evoke the common experience of all people in the inevitable sufferings of life. In the studio, we worked on layering the background vocals in a way that was artistic and unique. The hand of God seemed on those few days of recording at legendary Mama Joe's in North Hollywood.*

> *We finished the recording so quickly that we called up Phil Perkins and asked him to start to work on orchestrating the overdub sessions the very next day. Phil worked through the night, and into the recording session, literally writing charts as the songs were ready to record. Yet it all worked, and worked very well.* Hiding Place *remains one of my most requested recordings.* — JMT

It did not escape notice that Sr. Viola was at the heart and soul of these new developments. Through her prayers, selfless commitment to work, and vast experience in religious life, the groundwork had been laid for restructuring and renewal. With John Michael's leadership, and Viola's quiet, mature guidance, it was a partnership clearly ordained by God.

Their relationship was built on prayer as they contemplated their roles in the newly reforming community. Some of their shared prayer experiences seemed miraculous – minutes seemed like hours, hours seemed like minutes. Supernatural events occurred between them that are known only to John Michael and Viola, a spiritual director, and God. They were cautious and prudent in their moments together, always endeavoring to be upright examples of godly leadership to the community. But, clearly, something extraordinary was happening. They were happy as celibates, but God seemed to be altering their relationship as they spent an increasing amount of time together in prayer and discussion. However, they could not in good conscience counsel young and unformed celibates to "go and do likewise." Such amounts of time together have proven counterproductive to most new celibates who engage in it. God was forming a new kind of relationship between them. They began to consider what seemed inconsiderable: Is God calling us to marriage? They began a private process of discernment with spiritual direction.

Around this time John Michael and Viola made a discernment retreat at the place where it all began: Alverna. They sought the counsel of Fr. Martin on this matter through open and frank dialogue. Fr. Martin's advice was simple: they were legally free to marry by Church law, but it would not be without public repercussions that would ripple out a far distance. There would also be gossip.

During a time of deep prayer in the little Portiuncula Chapel John and the community had helped build, he went to the lectern that held the scriptures and opened the bible three times, just as he had done at the beginning of his vocational search at Alverna years before. The first was, "Have no fear about taking Mary as your wife. It is by the Holy Spirit that she has conceived this child. (Matthew 1:20)" The second was, "Should you marry, however, you will not be committing sin. (1 Corinthians 7:27)" The third was, "Lord, you know that I take this wife of mine not because of lust, but for a noble purpose (Tobit 8:7)" John knew that the child of the reformed community was birthed from Viola, that celibacy or marriage was a choice, and that God's will, not lust was the reason they would ever decide to marry. He felt that God had spoken directly through these scriptures.

Their marriage on February 17, 1989 seemed a logical progression to many but a shocking turn of events for others.

In 1988 John Michael had confided in close friends and in Fr. Martin Walter that he wondered if God might not be calling him to a marriage relationship to Sr. Viola. Having endured the taxing two-year process of annulment from his first marriage, and his private vows having expired, there was no objective religious reason why he could not remarry. Viola's vows as an Incarnate Word sister were already dispensed from Rome since her involvement in the new community. Seeking the advice of their bishops and spiritual leaders, the couple quietly entered a time of prayerful fasting and discernment in the quest for God's will and the appropriate permissions from church authorities. Bishop McDonald agreed to preside at a sacred wedding ceremony, and witness the vows for the Church.

It was a chilly, beautiful February evening. As darkness enveloped the cozy, Ozark monastic community, snowflakes began to fall gently, blanketing buildings and hillsides in a white mantle of blessing. In the newly constructed Charity Chapel, family, friends and community members gathered around the bishop and the expectant couple. One of John's best friends served as the best man and gave them the Heart–Tau necklaces they would exchange for life. John Michael Talbot and Viola Pratka became man and wife that night, an enduring partnership that would be marked by spiritual twists and turns and many trips around the world in missions of mercy, monastic outreach, and spiritual pilgrimages. This sacramental union gave them both a unique insight into both celibacy and marriage as the community that integrated both continued to unfold under their care by the power of God in the Church.

Today John Michael says that Viola has made him a better "monk," keeping in mind the wider definition given by St. John Chrysostum centuries ago, that all serious Christians are "monks" with no distinction, and that a married monastic tradition exists in some form or another in the various religions of the world. Ironically, the married monk phenomenon is part of most monastic expressions of the world's major religions. But it is not the normal expression in any of them. Of course, John Michael has never been anything but radical, despite his unquestioned obedience to God and the Church. He says, "she keeps me completely honest in the privacy of the Hermitage. There is no room to slacken in prayer or lifestyle. All must be for God, or not at all. Today I am living with a saint, and trying to have some of that saintliness run off on me through living together for God."

Mother Angelica

As soon as The Lord's Supper *and* Come to the Quiet *became well known, I was invited to appear at many Church conferences. I would frequently be asked to discuss my Catholic conversion. It was at a Charismatic Catholic conference in New Orleans that I first encountered Mother Angelica. People were excited because she had gotten a lot of attention with her show on a non-Catholic station in California. I found her presentation very humorous, but wished that she would share some of the deeper things from her background as a contemplative Poor Clare nun.*

I soon heard about the satellite dish at her monastery in Birmingham, and her new Catholic TV station. Bishop Law of Springfield urged me to put in a similar facility at our Little Portion Hermitage. I had seen too many similar ventures fail, so I respectfully declined.

Not long after, I was asked by Bishop Law to come up to Springfield Missouri with Dan and Cherry O'Neill, to speak about why we became Catholics, an event to be aired on Mother Angelica's new station. It was a smash success, and for a time, held the record for her most watched program. Sometime later, I appeared live on her talk show, and did some taped musical performances for later broadcast. These were equally well received.

But some trouble soon stirred. After the release of my book, The Fire of God, *a discreet inquiry was made by EWTN as to whether I was pro gay rights. I was a little shocked, having written the book to clearly present the teachings of the Church with enthusiasm. I had counseled one too many actively gay men interested in consecrated life, and I felt that it was time for a simple presentation of the Church's teaching regarding active homosexuality. Basically, it says to hate sin, but love the sinner. Many of those I counseled were*

> *ready to follow whatever the Church taught out of a genuine love of God, but they had simply never heard it presented in a clear and positive way. I clearly and lovingly presented the teaching of the Church on sexual ethics in that book. Requests for me to appear at EWTN abruptly ended.*
>
> *After Viola and I married, and Troubadour For The Lord was founded, we tried to buy advertising time on EWTN. We were refused on the basis that I was imitating a priest. Again, I was a bit stunned. My marriage was blessed by my own bishop, and the community Constitutions and Directories, containing a description of the community habit, were approved by the Church.*
>
> *Nevertheless, I think that God has used Mother Angelica in a powerful way. EWTN is the largest Catholic television network in America. What she does, she does very well. But her more archconservative theological opinions can never displace the true teaching authority of the Church.*
>
> — JMT

Earlier, many saw John Michael as an almost archetypical celibate monk. Countless novices and seminarians had been inspired by his example to enter consecrated monastic life, or to become ordained priests, themselves (though John was not a priest). Now John and Viola also became examples of radical monastic living in Catholic marriage as well. Through their own experience they became a paradoxical example for those called to both celibacy and marriage.

John Michael had given up his dream, and was given it back, though far deeper and richer than he could have conceived.

Expansion

One sunny Saturday afternoon after a neighborhood base-ball game, little Johnny Talbot noticed a neighbor trimming a tree with pruning hooks. A vast shower of twigs and branches fell at the foot of the apple tree in what appeared to be the destruction of a perfectly beautiful, well-established backyard fruit tree. "I will always remember how barren and even ugly that tree looked for the longest time. I thought it would surely die," John recalls. "But I will also remember the amazing explosion of growth and healthy fruit produced by that same tree the following year." This childhood image loomed large in John's mind and memory in a morning of quiet, contemplative prayer in the late '80s when he and community members seemed to be doing so much, yet accomplishing so little. Pruning! Cutting back ... We shall do it, he determined.

A year before they were married, and with Viola's energetic support, John went to work in the "orchard" of his community and began pruning. People were not pruned, but lifestyle certainly was. All unnecessary expenses were curtailed. Well-meaning but fruitless activities were cancelled. Prayer commitments were encouraged and expanded and, perhaps most startling of all, John took his own message to heart by canceling all concerts for the year. Some lost faith in John's leadership. Others became curious onlookers. But a remnant few saw the inherent wisdom of the pruning strategy. After all, John was tired, travel-weary, just flat tapped out. He had been carrying the responsibility and financial weight of the community on his shoulders for nearly a decade. He laid down his guitar and rested. And wondered. But it did not take long to see the spectacular results.

A sister spends time in adoration before the Blessed Sacrament in Charity Chapel. Adoration was started during the Gulf War, and has continued ever since.

One of the emerging characteristics of this Reform was integration. The community integrated all religion from a Christian base, all Christian faiths from a Catholic base, and all consecrated monastic expressions from a Franciscan base. Franciscanism was their mother, but they were a new spiritual child being born into the Church and into the world. They integrated the charismatic and the contemplative, the solitary and the communal, the spontaneous and the liturgical. Since they included every state of life, they integrated celibate, single, and family expressions. Also, a domestic expression included those who live in their own homes while embracing the spirit of the monastic cell. The evangelical counsels were professed by all in a way suitable to their state of life.

Because of the integration of families with the celibates, some accused the Reform of suspending religious commitments like chastity or poverty. But indeed the opposite was true. The Reform brought a greater religious discipline that was both a firm establishment of traditional monastic life for the celibate brothers and sisters, but in a way that also reached out and included families interested in a radical gospel alternative based on the monastic heritage in contrast to typical western life. The traditional commitments of poverty, chastity, and obedience were now clearly visible in a way appropriate for celibates, singles who were open to marriage, and in a way moderated for families.

This integration, coupled with a return to the roots of monastic and consecrated life, transformed the community into a unique expression of ancient consecrated life, and a possible sign of renewal and reform for the future of consecrated life in the Church. It had deep roots in the traditions of the past, and so was more prepared to grow higher in today's world as the church faces the challenges of the future.

John and Viola were soon invited to travel internationally to touch the lives of the poorest of the poor through Mercy Corps' global humanitarian mission in such poverty-stricken areas as Honduras, the Philippines and Palestinian refugee camps in the West Bank. These travels would later leverage outreach ministries in these very same regions when John and Viola dispatched community members and funding to assist disadvantaged children and families.

Not long before the Reform, a nearby retreat center at More Mountain suddenly became available at a surprisingly low price. The Episcopalian retreat facility had fallen on hard times and John had already considered sponsoring and directing retreats as a ministry of the monastery. The time was right. The retreat center was purchased and became a rallying point for conferences, meetings, and retreats led by a wide range of highly respected, spiritual retreat masters, including John. Since then, thousands have been drawn by John's retreats and by the ministry of many others at the retreat center since 1987. Today it is called The Little Portion Retreat and Training Center at More Mountain.

At the Hermitage, new buildings, including the beautifully simple Charity Chapel, a barn, greenhouses, a four-unit family residence, the Charity Medical Clinic, and the Common Center with offices and a library sprouted from the monastery grounds and in the nearby Eureka Springs community over a few short years. The buildings are monastic, Franciscan, and Ozark all at the same time. The covered walkways and beautiful prayer gardens and ponds are monastic and Franciscan. The wooden construction is Ozark, yet also looks like the famous wooden churches of the Eastern Rite in Russia. The spirituality of the Brothers and Sisters of Charity is seen to the knowing eye in the very buildings of the monastery. The Little Portion Hermitage seemed to blossom into a new Eden nestled in the quiet Ozark Mountains. Visitors from past years are often overwhelmed at the beauty of the present Little Portion Hermitage Monastery.

But they grew in numbers as well. The Hermitage community grew from about 5 to 50 in a little more than a year, and the Domestic expression, once called the Associates, likewise grew from 50 to 500. After the first energetic years of rapid growth the Hermitage would stabilize at around 30–40 members. The spiritual and human monastic "infrastructure" also began to take shape in new and exciting ways as new members were drawn to the monastery, and as new groups of Domestic members, or cell groups, began to form around the globe.

The newly finished Charity Chapel, built in 1989.

October 4, 1989 – Bishop Andrew J. McDonald blesses the new Charity Chapel, assisted by Deacon Sam Hillburn.

The Little Flower Health Clinic and Counseling Center, operated by the Brothers and Sisters of Charity.

A Sister makes her permanent profession into the hands of her spiritual mother, Viola Talbot, as John Michael witnesses.

1996 – As the General Minister of the community, John Michael prays over a brother entering the novitiate, an early stage of monastic life.

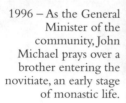

John Michael and Viola receive a family into postulancy at Little Portion.

Canonical Establishment/Fr. Alan McCoy

The Canonical, or legal, establishment of the Little Portion community in the Church was a long, and demanding process. It began with writing our charism and life on paper. The problem was that the community was young, and still developing. To write things too soon may deform its growth. To not write anything at all may leave it rudderless in the stormy seas of life in the Church and the world. Next, we had to pass it by the canon lawyers and vicars of religious of the Diocese. Their responsibility was to protect the Bishop from placing himself in civil or religious legal risk, while remaining open to new developments of the Spirit among the people of God. They literally questioned our community about everything. It was like running the gauntlet!

It is said that a founder of a community in the Church becomes a hack canon lawyer from this process. I found this to be true. I studied the Constitutions of many communities, both old and new, including Franciscans, Carmelites, Augustinians, and Benedictines, communities of the Christian East and West, and even non-Christian communities. I felt that the intellectual study was good, but it also kept me occupied with reading "about" monasticism, rather than living it. I saw that in some ways I was getting off track and beginning to burn out.

I finally thought, "Why am I doing all of this myself? If we hire civil lawyers, why don't we let a canon lawyer do this? They are the experts in canon law, not me!" I first contacted Fr. Basil Pennington, OCSO, who assembled an initial manuscript. We then contacted Fr. Alan McCoy, OFM, whom I had met at a conference of Franciscan hermitages at Graymore, New York.

Fr. Alan had a wealth of experience, having been the first president of the Canon Law Society of America, the first Executive Secretary of the Conference of Major Superiors of

Men in the US, a Provincial of the Santa Barbara Province of the Order of Friars Minor in the Western U.S., and a member of many delegations from the Franciscans to the Vatican concerning human rights and social justice issues around the world. His help proved to be invaluable, and he became a lasting friend to the community and me.

Between Fr. Alan and the leadership of the community, a document emerged from the manuscript that was approved without incident. We were approved as a Private Association of the Faithful first, and then, a few years later, were approved as a Public Association of the Faithful.

A Private Association is recognized by the Church, and must submit its Statutes to the Church for approval. A Public Association is approved and established by the Church, and represents the Church in its lifestyle, worship, and ministry. Fr. Alan felt that the community should become a public association, and we agreed. Fr. Alan became the community's official Visitor from the Bishop of Little Rock, and would help us in our initial development as a formal part of the Church.

This process also included travel to Rome for fact-finding and dialogue with the various leadership Councils and Congregations about the new community and its place in the overall Church. The result was great reception and encouragement by all. We discovered that we were not alone. About ten integrated monastic communities existed in the Church at the time, mostly in Europe, but we were the only one of this kind with Church approval in the United States. We learned a lifetime of encouraging facts in just a few days during each trip.

We were only surprised at one stop: The Council For the Laity. We had made an appointment months in advance, and expected a warm reception. What awaited us was a cold lesson in Roman protocol. Upon arriving at the correct office in Rome with several minutes to spare, we were told that we could not be seen that day. The Archbishop was too busy. They *said for us to try again tomorrow.*

We went back the next day, and were told the same thing. This time we didn't go away, but waited quietly in the outer office. Finally, after a few hours, the Bishop's lay secretary saw us. She proved to be a gold mine of information, and was very pleasant as we all looked through a picture album of the community and talked about the community's vision and lifestyle.

After she was convinced as to our worthiness, she ushered in the Archbishop. He came in and said curtly, "You wanted to see me, so here I am." It was clear that he wasn't in a pleasant mood. But after initial introductions he warmed up, and became friendly towards our small BSC community delegation. We returned from the trip greatly encouraged by the Spirit working through the Church.

We realized that God was bringing forth an ancient, yet new expression of integrated monasticism. A renewal of traditional religious life was forming through the combination of our celibate expressions, and a Catholic incorporation of family monasticism mainly from the Anabaptist tradition in recent centuries. Under the 1983 Code of Canon Law of the Church, new communities such as ours had to exist as public or private associations of the faithful, but it was time to prepare for a category that would truly house such communities in the future codes that inevitably come every century or so. It was exciting to be a part of such a radical development of consecrated life for celibates, and consecration of life for monastic families. ⸺ JMT

On December 6, 1990, Bishop Andrew J. McDonald officially recognized the community as a Private Association of the Faithful. Three years later, on October 4, 1993, the Feast Day of St. Francis of Assisi and the 10th anniversary of the establishment of The Little Portion Hermitage, Bishop McDonald's

John Michael and Viola
with Fr. Alan McCoy,
the community's first
Visitator.

letter officially proclaimed the community a Public Association
of the Faithful under the Catholic Diocese of Little Rock,
Arkansas. The community became the only integrated community of its type in North America to attain this status.

A Scripture Rule, Constitution, and Directories for each
expression of community membership mirrored ancient structures of lifestyle and government, but in a new way for this new
consecrated expression of integrated monastic community in
the Church. This established clear guidelines on the balance
between the authority of John Michael as the founder and spiritual father, whoever might succeed him, and the democratic
process of the permanent professed membership in General
Chapter, and the appointed or elected leaders in the General
Council. This legislative anchor was established at the same
time. In 1991 Fr. Alan McCoy, OFM, officially presided with
John Michael Talbot over the first General Chapter of Elections
for the leadership of the Brothers and Sisters of Charity, Domestic, thereby launching both monastic and domestic membership
dimensions of John Michael's long-held dream of community
and radical service to God through a collective pilgrimage of
faith which would ultimately span the globe.

In the spring of 1991, the Little Portion newsletter proclaimed through its headline, "GOD IS NOT DEAD—HE IS

ALIVE!" The fruit tree was exploding in new growth and much fruit. Monastic and domestic members of the community began traveling and serving the poor through their "ministry of presence" in Honduras, Jerusalem, and Nicaragua. A new monastic mission called, "Our Lady of the Angels Monastery" was established on the island of Ometepe in Lake Nicaragua, and in the Diocese of Granada, among some of the region's poorest peoples for the purpose of sharing a Gospel presence among orphans and the local poor.

Domestic and Monastic members of the Brothers and Sisters of Charity at the BSC's Our Lady of the Angels Monastery in Nicaragua.

Our Lady of the Angels Monastery's chapel and bell tower, and its crop of pitaya, a popular fruit in Nicaragua.

In spite of failing health which included sight problems, regular migraine headaches, and occasional bouts of self-doubt, John Michael's creative energy levels frequently spiked as was made apparent by many new record album projects, speaking engagements, a dizzying whirlwind of concert tours, and more than a dozen book projects. One wonders how he found the time and energy. But John and Viola Talbot know the answer: daily contemplative prayer and the predictable rhythms of monastic life at the beautiful Little Portion Hermitage monastery. Those cycles began to include regular and repeated prayer, work, retreats, itinerant prayer walks, community council meetings, annual gatherings of domestic members, conferences, recording projects, books, and a music outreach established through a new venture, Troubadour Productions.

"When I look at all that has transpired over these years in the way of outreach, ministry, projects—I myself am utterly amazed at how God has multiplied our simple faith in so many ways," John ponders. "But, in the end, strip it all away, and there is just one question at the heart of it all: will I simply and radically sell out to God and give up everything? The concerts, the monastery, the records, the recognition—everything?"

Viola reduces the issue to one simple word: obedience. "Are we willing to simply obey God?" she asks with a broad grin on her face and a sparkle in her eyes. You can tell she means serious business.

It was about this time that John Michael received a dream that he believed to be from God. In the dream he entered a big rehearsal room in an old castle-like house. Once inside he found a very popular Christian Contemporary band rehearsing. The band wanted John to join them, but he had to give up his monastic habit, wear running shorts, and play an electric guitar. John declined, and the band began to try to convince him that his Catholic/Franciscan path was not from God. At this point an angel with a broken hand flew down from a huge vaulted ceiling, took John by the arm, and flew him to the very top of the ceiling, some ten or twenty floors up. John remembers looking down at his dangling sandaled feet and the flowing habit as he ascended upwards with ease because of the help of the angel. John understood that the broken handed angel represented God's grace through brokenness, and that he would only "fly" through realizing his own brokenness and relying on God entirely.

The angel took John Michael to a little ready room with a view out over a huge expanse of hundreds of thousands of people. He was supposed to share his gift and minister to the huge crowd. It would be a few years later that John would experience the literal fulfillment of the dream while ministering in conjunction with the Papal visits of Pope John Paul II to the Untied States. Specifically, World Youth Day 2000 in Denver seemed a most exact fulfillment when John Ministered to over 500,000 people that stretched from the main stage to the horizon of Cherry Creek park, where the main papal events took place.

Sometimes God gives special and unexpected rewards. In 1991, I was fortunate to accompany John Michael, Viola, and the community's official Visitor, Fr. Alan McCoy, to Rome where they attended meetings with Vatican authorities. In a dizzying series of meetings, they met with bishops, archbishops, cardinals, brothers and sisters, and officials from various religious communities. They even shared lunch with the Minister General of the Franciscans. One night in their hotel room, they received a phone call: "Be at St. Peter's Square, at a designated door, at 5:30 AM. You are to be included in the Pope's private mass."

The next morning after walking through the chilly air past the Swiss guards at St. Peter's Square, the four of us were ushered into the Pope's private chapel to celebrate Mass and personally receive the Eucharist from Pope John Paul II in an unforgettable moment that, for us, will last forever. John and Viola left Rome with a new fire and confirmation from the successor to St. Peter, and the Vicar of Christ on earth in today's modern world.

Papal Visits

I have had the privilege to sing for many papal events, but I have only met him once. With the approval of our Bishop we went to Rome for some visits with the various offices and leaders concerning the proper formation of a new community in the Church. We had also arranged for a possible meeting with the Pope through Cardinal Law. By the last couple of days in

Rome the meetings had all gone well, but we had all but given up hope for a papal meeting. Then we received a call from the Papal Secretary: Be at a certain entrance at St. Peter's Square at 5:00 AM the next day.

The next day was a bitter cold December morning in Rome. It was icy and dark. We got to St. Peter's, and there was simply nobody there. What a difference from the bustling crowd we usually encountered. We waited outside for some time before others began to appear, equally cold, but equally excited.

After what seemed an eternity, Swiss Guards invited us all in. Once inside, we removed our winter jackets and scarves, and were led through a virtual maze of ornately decorated hallways and across an outdoor quadrangle. As soon as we were thoroughly confused as to our actual position in the Papal wing of the Vatican, we suddenly found ourselves in the Papal Chapel.

The Pope was already there, totally absorbed in intense prayer. We all joined him while the visiting priests vested and came out into the front chairs. Next, some sisters and acolytes vested him as he knelt, and then stood. I thought to myself, he has lost all personal ego. He isn't even allowed to vest himself as most priests and bishops do throughout the Church.

Mass began. It was a completely ordinary Mass. The singing was spirited, but just as out of tune, as ordinary masses at most parishes. I thought to myself: even in the Vatican the masses are just like everywhere else. It is the presence of Jesus that makes the Mass special, not the performance.

The only thing unusual about the Mass was the time for silent prayer. There was no homily, and no intercessions. There was only prayerful, intense silence. We had ten minutes in place of the homily, ten minutes in place of the intercessions, and another ten minutes after Holy Communion. I was overwhelmed, but also very comfortable. I felt as if I were experiencing Mass for the first time, however, nothing unusual was *occurring externally. The specialty was purely spiritual.*

Finally, it was time for Communion. We filed out of our row of seats toward the Holy Father. I was about to receive Communion from the Vicar of Christ and the successor to St. Peter. My knees trembled—I was overwhelmed.

It was then that I realized that it was something even greater than this that occurs at every Mass—It is Jesus Himself who is present in the Eucharist, not merely his servant. I learned many lessons I thought I already learned without a word being said at that Liturgy.

After the Mass we were escorted into a large reception room to meet the Pope. He made his way around to the some fifty people, finally reaching us. We shared briefly about our community, my ministry, and Mercy Corps. He simply said, but with great seriousness and conviction, "God bless your new community." We left with the sense that Jesus had spoken directly to us that day.   ⌐ JMT

Over the years, John Michael again encountered the Pope when he played his guitar and sang at World Youth Day in Toronto in 2002. He was also invited to the Inaugural Prayer Luncheon after the election of George W. Bush as President of the United States in 2001. John has also received a Dove Award from the Gospel Music Association, prestigious literary awards for his books, played for Mother Teresa of Calcutta, received Mercy Corps' Humanitarian of the Year Award, and has received countless other citations for his music and ministry. Religious and secular news programs have aired stories about John Michael Talbot and the community. ABC's "Good Morning America," People Magazine, and the Wall Street Journal newspaper were among the many who reported on this musician and his religious community. The more he tried to disappear into solitude and silence, the more publicity kept coming to him unsolicited.

In spite of the praise, rewards, accolades, and citations, singer-songwriter-guitarist-author-teacher-spiritual leader, John Michael Talbot will still quietly retreat to his dressing room after an exhausting three-hour concert and ask, "Did I do okay? Did I stumble? Do you think I really ministered to the people?" He then retreats, exhausted, to his hotel room yet one more night. One more of thousands. Even then, he asks Viola if he met expectations. That a man so amazingly accomplished in his art and his craft, and so recognized by his peers, with broad affirmation from his constituents, should ask such questions is, indeed, a mystery.

But one thing is abundantly clear after the pruning that had begun years ago – it worked.

Trials and Crucibles

Despite the wonderful miracles and many confirmations from God, the community continued to face the very real challenges of living in the civilization of the modern west. Many came, and many still left after weeks, months, or years. The community had encountered that demon of American society: Individualism.

Traditional Christianity values individuation, or the reverence for the uniqueness and non-repeatability of each living thing, especially human life. Individualism is individuation gone bad. One brings a wonderful reverence for life. The other produces a culture of the primacy of self. When individualism becomes the norm, none of the traditional structures of human society can remain standing for many generations. Families fall apart, church communities experience the revolving door syndrome, the work place becomes overly competitive and unstable, and the unborn are "terminated" if they are unwanted, or thought too inconvenient. The "me centered society" becomes the "culture of death" that John Paul II has so prophetically proclaimed of the west.

"At first when people would leave we would rationalize

that it was because of our self-centered culture of individualism and death. We would tend to just draw the line of Catholic Christianity more deeply in the sand and hunker down with greater determination. We would try to be just a bit more enthusiastic in our gospel way of life. But soon we discovered that this does not work either, failing to solve the deeper problems in the human hearts of those who stay. We were failing to look within. The result was blaming the external for emerging problems. External answers are superficial. Those in leadership began to wear out," John recalls.

John Michael now believes that he also unavoidably fell victim to the pattern of the primary leader taking the hit for complaints against the community or the Church. This was further compounded when those with pre-existing authority issues tried to make it in the monastic community which by its nature values obedience to legitimate authority as a way of letting go of the old false self. John Michael says, "If they do not really let go of that old person, the very structure and lifestyle become something that seems too oppressive. Without a radical change within, they would have to leave." But in order to leave with "legitimacy" they had to find something wrong with the community, which usually means criticizing the leadership. It becomes a passive/aggressive love/hate relationship leading to anger, resentment, and the bitterness.

St. John Cassian mentions an avaricious monk who is both tragically humorous, and frighteningly similar to modern community experiences of those who leave, and the interior psychology and external steps from seemingly insignificant problems to major acts of division on the part of some who do.

John Michael also began to find his own modern experience in the descriptions of the monastic founders from 800–1700 years ago. Contrary to popular opinion, after the initial inner tranquility, and outer solitude of the founder's personal life as a hermit, the beginnings of monastic foundations often got off to very turbulent starts. St Pachomius had to confront the first batch of recruits who refused to take the life seriously by actually living the monastic life of gospel sacrifice and asceticism. St. Benedict was almost poisoned to death by the first monks, who asked him to leave the hermit's life and direct their lukewarm monastery. He was also later resisted, falsely accused, and almost poisoned once more by a local priest. The same monks who had asked him to reform their monastery in the role of Abbot also threatened St. Romuald. This pattern is well established, and not terribly surprising for the veteran monastic. Today we do not poison our founders physically. We do it by gossip, slander, and character assassination.

Brother to Brother/Christian Ecumenism

The Brother to Brother *project with Mike Card started with me asking him to sing background vocals on my* Wisdom *recording. My friends had often said that Michael Card is an evangelical version of me, and that we should do a joint project.*

During the Wisdom *sessions, Mike was the one who actually brought up the subject of doing a joint album. He said, "I'll do my favorite songs of yours, and you do the songs of mine that you like." It was a winning suggestion. I found freshness in his songs, and used some alternative arrangements from the ones Mike had used on his recordings. He did the same with mine. The resulting sessions were creative and fun, and the music reflected this optimistic spirit.*

In spite of some anti-Catholic criticism aimed at Mike during the Brother to Brother *concert tour, the concerts were an exhilarating success. We two brothers in Christ won over the audiences throughout the country.*

I grew to respect Mike for taking so much heat during that period. I did not receive much because Catholic teaching is

> *clear about Christian ecumenism. I was just following the*
> *teaching of the Catholic Church. Unfortunately, Mike did not*
> *have that same support. Today, Mike and I remain dear co-*
> *workers and friends.* —JMT

As with many of today's religious, secular, and public figures, John Michael's leadership has occasionally been questioned, resulting in community and Church inquiries and investigations. These inquiries fall within the competency of a confidential pastoral process of the community and the Church. But they can be uncomfortable for all involved. John Michael has always been found to be a competent leader, a faithful Catholic Christian and community founder. However, these experiences understandably wear a leader down through the years. John Michael was no exception.

Ironically, it was one who criticized the most who, in a

This 1996 photo was from the *Brother to Brother* series.
John Michael notes, "...getting grayer."

dream saw John Michael dwelling peacefully with a small group of hermits dressed in primitive monastic garb. Suddenly, John Michael was called away from the hermitage to respond to accusers. When he returned to the peace of the hermitage, he would be physically exhausted, but spiritually illuminated. The subsequent events proved this dream prophetic.

As John Michael now says, "I began to see myself like a rag doll, it's stuffing knocked out. Ultimately the doll becomes emptied of itself. What was left was an empty space in which Jesus could dwell without resistance. True freedom is then achieved." In that sense, the trials John Michael suffered eventually made him a stronger follower of Jesus Christ. He was learning to die to the remnants of self that had yet to be conquered in his spiritual life. This lesson can only be learned with time, patience, and faith.

"This is where a third paradoxical word came in: 'Build community by not building community.' I realized that my enthusiasm about what God was doing in our midst in the initial days of the Reform was eclipsing the contemplative dimension of my own life. I can now see I overcompensated in the Reform. I also discovered that for the average American, a message as radical as ours was already forceful enough on its own. I was inadvertently rolling over people with my enthusiasm, and I was getting physically sick from the emotional burnout," says John Michael today.

John sensed another still small voice from God at that time of trial: "It is your job to make the community available. It is mine (God's) to make it succeed." A huge weight lifted from John Michael's shoulders. John had only to fulfill his role as founder and leader. This is not unlike the word given to St. Francis 800 years ago when God asked Francis, "Whose community is this, yours or mine?" Francis replied that it was God's, not his. Francis experienced a great release in that simple admission. From that time forward John would say that he would simply live the life to which God had called him. If others wished, they were free to follow. If not, he would happily walk the spiritual path alone. John was being set free.

Lessons of St. Francis

After authoring numerous books for the Christian Bookseller's Association (CBA) and Catholic stores, I was handed a whole new approach, almost on a platter. Steve Rabey, a distinguished professional writer who had previously invited me to a national conference of the Evangelical Press Association, called about doing a book about St. Francis for the general religious readers that shop at larger chain bookstores. I was interested, because I was also aware of the growing numbers of religious seekers.

After an agreement was signed with Putnam, Steve and I began a serious period of writing and dialoguing. Steve had come from a scholarly evangelical perspective, and I had the experience of life in a new integrated Franciscan/monastic community in the Catholic Church. The book received critical acclaim for its integrated balance between the two traditions, and was a big seller. It also began a long friendship between Steve and I.

I then began to realize that I had the opportunity to write for a wider range of readers than I had previously encountered in the strict CBA and Catholic bookstore customers. Most religious readers were becoming disinterested in the New Age movement, and wanted to learn about mysticism that was rooted in solid tradition. This was evident in the success of monastic books and recordings from many different world religions.

It was then that I began to share my faith in Christ from the perspective of life in the Catholic Church and the monastic community in an inclusive, yet uncompromising way. It also led me to express the teachings and practice of the Church and her monastic expressions concerning interfaith dialogue.

~JMT

John recommitted himself to daily meditation, which had originally drawn him to the Catholic Church. This included the contemplative traditions from the Christian East and West, and interfaith resources. He read a book on the American experience of Buddhist monasticism in the face of the individualism of the west, in which he observed the same struggles of founding and maintaining monastic life in North America. The following exercise highlight from John's book on Christian meditation, *Come to the Quiet*, describes his approach.

The centrality of the Christian Faith is the Cross and Resurrection of Jesus Christ, the Paschal Mystery. For us it is more than the paradox of the mystics of the other great faiths. For us it is not a teaching, or even an experience to be gained by meditation practitioners, though it includes this as well. For us it EXISTS beyond teaching in the person of Jesus, the Way, the truth, and the Life. Genuine Christian meditation must, then, lead us to the actual experience of this Mystery if it is to be truly Christian.

1) Begin as in the other meditations: Sit in your meditation space. Breathe deeply to settle and still your senses of the body, emotions and thoughts of the soul, and be aware of your spirit in the Spirit of God.

2) After breathing deeply, be aware of your body and the senses. Thank God for them as gifts

from God. Be aware of the awesome wonder of their interconnectedness with the rest of creation, starting with your parents and family, and reaching out to the earth and all life that springs from it. Then, be aware that, despite the wonder of the body, it is only our temporary home during this lifetime. It will grow old, degenerate, and die. After that, it will decompose in the grave. It will be resurrected, but in a whole new, and more wonderful form. Also be aware that, in this fallen world, the disordered sensual self is sometimes a cause of great trouble and pain to the soul. So we bring the body, and all that it is, to the Cross of Christ, and let it go. By doing this all that is dysfunctional and out of order on our body more naturally finds its place in the will of God, and we know peace. We know the first fruits of Resurrection and new life even in this temporary home of the body.

3) Next, move to the emotions of the body and soul. Go through the same steps as with the senses of the body. Be aware of the gift they are from God, and thank God for them. Know that they are interdependent and conditioned by the other things of this phenomenal world. If we experience pleasure we are peaceful and happy. If things do not go as we want, we are agitated and unhappy. Know that they are also temporary, and impermanent. As conditions change, so do our emotions change. They come and go, rise and fall, with the changing of conditions in our life. They are part of us, but they are not the deepest being of who we really are. So, we can relax and peacefully bring them to the Cross of

Jesus. This brings greater peace as we now experience the emotions as they were originally intended to function, as mobilizers of the things of God and good in our life.

4) Next, we come to our thoughts. As with senses and emotions, we first acknowledge the thoughts today. Are they negative or positive, clear or unclear, confused or focused? We thank God for the gift of the thoughts and cognition of our spiritual mind. Then we realize that thoughts come and go. They are positive today, negative tomorrow, depending upon what conditions of the phenomenal world affect them. We have thoughts, but we are not our thoughts. Our deepest self is much deeper. So, we bring our thoughts to the Cross of Christ and let them go. As we do this we can sense them draining away from us, along with the tension and stress they often cause. We are reborn in the Resurrection of Christ through this process.

5) Lastly, having let go of the senses, emotions, and thoughts that so often agitate us, we become intuitively aware of our spirit in God's Spirit, essence to Essence, Breath to Breath. Simply breathe in this wonderful union with the deepest Essence of God beyond all thoughts, emotions, or sensual perceptions, yet building and empowering them all. Take some quality and unhurried time to simply BE here. Breathe the awakening of your spirit in the Spirit of God.

6) After some quality time in the place of spirit, conclude as in the other meditations, having first thanked God for any graces received.

Cave of the Heart/Interfaith

After the Brother to Brother *project, I wrote an even more contemporary work that reflected the mystical tradition of other major religions within the teaching of the Catholic church called* Cave of the Heart. *I've heard that the collection is considered by many to be one of my most creatively inspired musical pieces in recent years. We included an integration of contemporary folk, rock, and classical musical styles, and we used texts from major religions of the world, presenting Jesus Christ as the complement and fulfillment of all that is good in the religious longings of humankind.*

Unfortunately, the interfaith sensitivity in the lyrics kept the work from being accepted by Christian adult contemporary radio, and its listeners. Catholics found no problem with it, for the album correctly reflected the teaching of the Church. Today I'm not surprised. We took a risk in doing something radical, and I am glad that my Catholic listeners liked it. It just didn't work with the more conservative non-Catholic listener. Sometimes you win, sometimes you lose, and there are never any guarantees.

The accompanying book was a different story, though. I wrote Music of Creation *as an in-depth presentation of the orthodox Catholic faith for the religious seeker searching through the aisles of the large bookstores across America. Like* Cave of the Heart, *it was sensitive to the truth and goodness found in other religions, without compromising the uniqueness of Jesus Christ, or the Catholic Church.*

We did a tour of five big Borders Bookstores in five major cities. We had audiences of two or three hundred at most stores, and I did a song, shared about Jesus as the complement and completion of the human search for God. Then we did Q and A. The questions were great. It provided me the opportunity to get closer to readers and listeners in a more informal setting. I wish that we had taped it for TV. It would have made a great series.

~ JMT

Longtime friend and producer Phil Perkins, engineer Brent King and John Michael listen intently to the final mix of *Cave of the Heart*.

In the light of Church teaching, John Michael began to incorporate eastern practices of meditation into his life and in the community. He gained a new understanding of how to bring the gospel of Jesus to those who practice eastern faiths in a way they could understand. In resuming daily mediation his health slowly improved and stabilized. His leadership was re-kindled from a much deeper place of peace and calm in Christ. John was gaining the wisdom that only comes from experience.

Some complained about this integration of non-Christian religious ideas, but John clearly followed the conservative teachings of the Church and the legislation of the community. The Church says specifically:

"The Catholic Church rejects nothing that is true and holy in these religions. She regards with sincere reverence those ways of conduct and of life, those precepts and teachings which, though differing in many aspects from the ones she holds and sets forth, nonetheless often reflect a ray of that Truth which enlightens all men. Indeed, she proclaims, and ever must proclaim Christ "the way, the truth, and the life" (John 14:6) (Declaration on the Relation of the Church to Non-Christian Religions, Nostra Aetate, Number 2)"

Through testing and trials, John Michael grew into a mature teacher of simple living, charismatic gifts, and deeper contemplation. He earned his gray beard the hard way—through the crucible of community. As he says, "I am far from perfect, but on balance, I do all right."

Community members also learned some valuable lessons. As John Michael repeatedly proclaims, "More are called to community than come, and more are called to stay than do. But when they leave we do not send out failed brothers or sisters of charity. We send out better Christians." This idea lifted the sense of sadness and guilt that the community felt when a member decided to leave. Only rarely has a member been asked to leave. Most who leave eventually reconcile.

The renewed practice of Christian meditation caused him to be able to look lovingly and with genuine forgiveness to all those who had hurt him or community members, especially those who had left the community with anger and bitterness. But it also enabled John with the greatest freedom from self and pride; the ability to ask forgiveness easily. This is the last stronghold of ego, and it was a great relief to John Michael to let that bastion completely fall.

The changes in John Michael were not only internal. They also affected his external actions. In 2000, after the example of Pope John Paul II, and after having done so privately on many occasions, John Michael spoke on behalf of himself and the community in publicly offering and asking forgiveness from past and present members who may have been hurt in some way through his or the community's actions.

Repent, Reconcile, Rejoice!

On the occasion of this Jubilee year Pope John Paul II, and various individuals, and conferences of Bishops have released letters asking forgiveness for the various sins and oversights of the Church universal, and in her particular expressions. They have done so to follow, and enter fully into the teaching of Jesus on forgiveness and reconciliation. In this spirit of reconciliation during the great Jubilee, after their holy examples, and for the same reason, I now do the same as General Minister of The Brothers and Sisters of Charity at Little Portion Hermitage, both personally, and on behalf of the whole community.

For any and all sins committed by myself personally, or by any leaders, or members as a whole, against community members past or present, or those outside the community, committed knowingly, or unknowingly, I would humbly and sincerely ask forgiveness. I try to follow Jesus daily, but there are many times when I still fail. I think I speak for the whole community in this. On behalf of all and myself, I ask forgiveness. Regarding some more specific ways, among others, I have always had a burden for past community members. I think this is normal for anyone in leadership. Some simply leave because this life is not for them.

But others leave unhappy about something, otherwise, why would they want to leave? Most all have been offered and have received forgiveness. Likewise they have offered it in return, and it has been graciously received. Yet, some may still harbor bitterness in the heart. Especially for these, let me again ask, and offer, forgiveness for any sin through misunderstanding or hurt.

Through all of this most of us really try to follow Jesus, and His way, truth, and life of selflessness, which opens a whole new way of life free of the hurt and anger that come from preoccupation with self. But because we are frail and fragile human beings, we do not always succeed. We stay trapped in the self, and so feelings get hurt when things do not go our way. Then we get angry. Then comes misunderstanding as we try to justify ourselves. Then come the disagreements and divisions in community. Lastly, this all settles into a deep-set bitterness that poisons everything in our life. This is the well-known and tragic age-old pattern. As St. Paul says so poignantly, "The things I want to do, I do not, and the things I do not want to do, I do. Who will deliver me from this body of death?" But he goes on in his letter to the Romans to show us a way out through death to the old self and the appearing of a new person conformed to the image of Christ through the cross and resurrection of Jesus. This is good news, indeed!

But there is more. I also ask forgiveness for the times when we have really tried to operate without the old self, but still made the wrong objective decisions on specific issues. These are not all known to us at the time, or even during this lifetime, despite the sharing of other opinions by those who disagree. They usually remain simple differences of opinion. I am sure the Lord will bring many of these to light when we see him face-to-face! For these times I ask forgiveness. Of course, sin and forgiveness is not just about objective mistakes, or our own personal spiritual growth program. It is about people. It is a matter of the heart. Sin and lack of forgiveness hurt people. It breaks hearts, and the heart of God. Especially in leadership, *we try to keep the human dynamic at the forefront of any communal decision, but sometimes we fail, or even this is not enough to keep people from being hurt. For all these times we ask forgiveness.*

It has been said that the battle for the soul is in the mind. In my own thoughts I always try to think of those with whom I still need reconciliation in a positive light. But more than this, I try to spiritually intuit fondly, kindly, and compassionately toward all who have harmed me, or think I intentionally harmed them. Even if there are external differences between us, I try to communicate with them on the level of the human spirit in God's Spirit, where we can really reach the essence of one another in the Essence of God. Here we reach past the peripherals of life, which so often divide us, to the deepest spirit of humanity in God's Spirit where we can be fully united in Divine love and communion heart to heart. For the times we have failed to do this I ask forgiveness.

So let's have done with all the old grudges and divisions, and, "bury the hatchet," as the old saying has it. Let's truly let go of our old self so that we can repent of our own sin, and be ready to offer forgiveness to any and all brothers and sisters who have sinned against us. In our deepest hearts we all desire reconciliation through Christ with anyone with whom we still need healing. Through this letter, let the healing begin! May the Lord grant you peace. — JMT

From the October, 2000 BSC Newsletter

The integration of monastic life and meditation practices of other faiths revived yet another feature of the original vision from years past: itinerant mendicancy. Within the traditions of the Sannyasins of Hinduism, the mendicant monks of Buddhism, and the wandering Sages and Wayfarers of Taoism/Confucianism, John Michael found another ancient confirmation of his vision of wandering from parish to parish on foot. The scriptures clearly include this in the life of Jesus and his disciples, apostles, early itinerants, and later monastic reformers such as St. Romuald, the founder of the of the Camaldolese Hermits. This way of life was a hallmark of John's favorite saint, St. Francis of Assisi.

John and the community began to do itinerant walks in total poverty, prayer, and availability. This occurred with Viola's prodding. During the first year of the Reform, around the Feast of St. Francis, (October 4th) Viola exclaimed, "Stop talking about it, and just do it!" The next day, John and Viola led a small band on foot from Little Portion Hermitage to Little Rock, Arkansas.

"It was over 150 miles, with no agenda and no money except the ten dollars in each one's pocket to avoid vagrancy charges. The team would show up at a Catholic or non Catholic church and say, "We're here. We will do whatever you want. We will do manual labor, visit your sick, lead worship, assist with programs, or whatever else would be of service to the local church community. We will also leave if that is what you want."

"During these walks we learned lessons that cannot be taught in books or monasteries. You learn how to be poor, which makes you truly grateful for the smallest gift from a benefactor. I remember one particularity hot autumn day on that walk. The sun was beating down, and there was no shade, or much room to walk on the side of the road. A truck drove past slowly, and the driver stared hard at us. We thought we could be in for trouble. Then, a few minutes later he returned with a bag of peaches. We savored those peaches! Never had a peach tasted so good. Since then it is impossible for me to eat one without true gratitude," John says with a smile.

The community began doing more prayer walks in other cities, geared more for local participants, often elderly, or infirm.

In this model they would walk from one church to another, usually covering a few miles at most. The practice was to walk slowly in contemplative, peaceful prayer through the often-troubled cities of America. With each step, the prayer walk group receives the blessing of the forefathers and mothers of faith who walked there before, bringing new blessings of faith during the walk. The walk includes a form of breath–prayer, so that each step, and each breath, becomes a prayer and a blessing from God.

The Prayer Walks have been successful in major cities, including San Francisco, San Diego, Philadelphia, Scranton, St. Louis, Kansas City, and others. It is one of John Michael's long held dreams to repeat the walks in the historic religious places of America, such as the California Missions, historic monasteries, shrines, and cathedrals.

Eve Weiss, the Domestic General Minister of the Brothers and Sisters of Charity, with John Michael on a prayer walk in Harrisburg, Pennsylvania in 2001.

John Michael began to experience the universal monasticism prophesied by St. Bonaventure some seven hundred years ago when he spoke of a time when a Universal Seraphic Order, including, but not limited to, existing religious communities like the Franciscans, Dominicans, Augustinian Canons, or Benedictines, would help to raise up a contemplative Church of the future from the midst of great persecution and trial. It is to this expression of community that John Michael feels most drawn. Consequently, the Brothers and Sisters of Charity embraced the role of the Desert Fathers and Mothers and all monastic traditions that flowed out of that phenomenal beginning in the deserts of Egypt so many centuries ago.

To help facilitate this vision of universal monasticism, the use of Benedictine retreat masters became a practice. Through the years Cistercian Abbot Basil Pennington, OCSO, of Conyers Georgia, Abbot Jerome Kodell, OSB, from Arkansas' own Subiaco Abbey, and Monsignor Franck Chiodo from a new Benedictine community in Iowa directed retreats at Little Portion. Sr. Perpetua Hawes, IWS, Viola's Reverend Mother from her days with the Incarnate Word Sisters of the Blessed Sacrament, gave a beautiful retreat hearkening back to Viola's Augustinian religious formation. Of course the input of those like Fr. Alan McCoy, OFM, the community's last saintly Visitator, has left a permanent mark on the community's spirituality and lifestyle.

The legislation for the community in the Monastic Directory of the Brothers and Sisters of Charity says, "Regarding personal imitation of Christ and apostolic ministry, we find primary inspiration from St. Francis. Regarding orderly community life in the integrated monastery, we find our greatest inspiration from the Rule of St. Benedict. Of course, the Desert Fathers and Mothers who preceded them both is of great importance as an in inspiration for our life." The Constitutions and Directories of the community are replete with references to all the monastic streams in the desert of gospel living.

Simplicity / Come Worship the Lord / Chant from the Hermitage

As our community settled into the life of the Reform, it took on a special charism beyond the integrations of spiritualities, monastic and Franciscan charism, and states of life. It became a steady beacon of hope for those who were seeking simple living for all states of the Christian lifestyle in the midst of a complicated world. Dan O'Neill and I put the core ideas into writing with the book, Simplicity. *It seemed to strike a chord in the consciousness of thousands. The book was followed by* Simplicity *retreats at the Little Portion Retreat Center, and Schools for Simple Living at the Hermitage. People came from all across the U.S. to experience a taste of a simpler lifestyle. They studied, worked in the monastery gardens, and did service work door to door in our neighboring towns. Most all were able to take something of substance back home with them. It was very successful, showing just how open people are to the simple life.*

Two recordings portrayed the simple charismatic and liturgical worship services at the Hermitage. The first was a two CD series called, Come Worship the Lord, *and captured the raw energy of charismatic praise in the monastic Charity Chapel. The recording was left very simple and unadorned, to depict the almost primitive character of the worship of the community. It did not have the polish of the many best selling worship and praise recordings of the non-Catholic mega churches, but we didn't want that as a musical representation of a community dedicated to simplicity. Though it never set sales records,* Come Worship the Lord *continues to guide many toward radical conversion to God in Christ and the Church.*

The second recording, Chant from the Hermitage, *depicted the monastic chant of the community. Taking the Morning and Evening Prayer chants that we used for years in daily common prayer, this chant is simple and haunting. It is more complex than much of the chant that is used by consecrated communities today, yet it remains simple enough for a community of average voices to learn and use.*

After the recording had been out for a while, I received a letter from France. It was from the St Peter's Abbey at Solesmes, which is famous for its resurrection of authentic Gregorian chant for liturgical use in the monasteries and churches of today. The writer said that he considered the chant of Little Portion to be one of the best attempts to translate the authentic Gregorian chant for the Liturgy of the Hours into modern English. Each language has its own flow and meter, and the music for one language is not always good for another. English has always required something unique, and no one has ever really gotten English chant right. It was an honor to receive encouragement and praise from such an honored source.

— JMT

The full dimension of the original vision began to unfold very naturally after the Reform of the late 1980s, but it did not come easily or without great price. With every victory there were many hard lessons and disappointments. For every person who stayed, nearly ten would come and go. And behind every recording project, there were hundreds of hours of work, and months of touring. It has taken a toll on John Michael and Viola, who have paid a high price for obedience to God's call. John readily states that in today's society, it takes a sustained miracle for a monastic community to work in America, especially the new ones. Countless communities have risen only to fade away after a few short years. One thing is certain: The Brothers and Sisters of Charity are still here, living a radical counter cultural gospel life of obedience, poverty and chastity.

John recalls an encounter with Fr. Richard Rohr, a

respected teacher and retreat master. They met in the lobby of a West Coast hotel shuttling back and forth from a nearby Catholic men's conference. Fr. Richard approached John Michael with great enthusiasm and said, encouragingly, "You're still at it." It was true. So many have come and gone. John Michael Talbot and the Brothers and Sisters of Charity are still ministering, still praying, still serving. Still here.

The Music Lives

~~~~~

The Birth of Jesus

In the more classical choral tradition, we put together The Birth of Jesus, *a Christmas celebration. We used about half old Christmas Carols and half new songs of mine. We used a large orchestra, and a mixed adult and boys choir from England. It was recorded at Angel Studios in London. This album is one of the joys of my recording career.*

The boys' choir was delightful. During the session they were the model of discipline and excellence. The headmaster was with us in the control room, and knew precisely what they were capable of and what we should watch for. At the break this choir of little professionals became regular kids again. They were all curious about a real recording studio, and smiled ear to ear as we gave them the grand tour, and explained the equipment and procedures. Then, Viola had the idea to give them some money for treats across the street at the market. As they ran and yelped on their dash towards the candy shelves, even the headmaster chuckled at the innocent, and fun-filled sight.

I also remember the adult choir. They were seasoned professionals, and had been used for such sound track recordings as

The Mission. *They sang beautifully in the morning. But when they came back from their lunch break at the nearby pub, they were a bit tipsy from the ale. As they sang "O Come All Ye Faithful," the slurring of the words was audible. Yet, due to tight time schedules we had no choice but to keep the take. It is clearly audible on the recording, and makes me smile and wince a bit to this day. I can only hope that some of the meaning of the words got through to the professional singers as they performed!* ⁓ JMT

Throughout the remarkable story of John Michael Talbot there have been many celebrated "firsts". John's first guitar, his first concert, the first recording, the first road tour, the first time Mason Proffit band members heard one of their records on the radio, the first time this young man sensed the powerful presence of God in his life, his first Christian album, the first of countless awards, the first day a real community was established, the first public prayer walk, the first official visit to The Vatican—these, and many more firsts have been chronicled in journals, diaries, newsletters, books and articles. Not all firsts, however, are quite so joyful.

In the quiet, mysterious days between Christmas and New Years in 1996, the very first grave was being prepared at the monastery grounds. The cemetery had been created for others more advanced in age, but as they say, the first monastic grave is never for whom you think. Today, beneath a simple marker and Ozark earth, lie the earthly remains of John's mother, Jamie Talbot. Born November 21, 1919. Died December 26, 1996.

Jamie had lived an intense life, punctuated by family crises, illness, joys, and spiritual triumphs. In her final years, her most blessed moments were spent at the monastery where she was professed as a full member in 1989. She was the resident "mom" and seamstress, sewing all of the community's habits, prayer shawls, shirts and pants.

"That day after Christmas, we visited her in the hospital where she was recovering from an operation, but we knew she was failing," John recalls. "I sang to her. She knew I was there and was present to us for a few special moments. Then she slipped away. We gave her to God." It was little Johnny's music that caught Jamie's attention in a special way nearly four decades earlier. It would be John's quiet music that would again touch her soul on her deathbed.

Over the years many things had changed—cycles of birth, death, crisis and renewal. But throughout a lifetime, one thing has remained the same for those closely associated with John Michael Talbot. The spiritual power of his music.

"Ironically, it was at that time that we began getting numerous reports and letters from those who used the music God has given through me to play as a loved one passes from this life to the next. I was aware of people using the music for baptisms, weddings, even childbirth. But nothing could prepare me for this use of my music. To think that someone would want to hear these simple songs as they go from their loved ones to God? It was completely overwhelming to me, and still is to this day," John Michael whispers reverently.

It was with a sense of blessed resignation that John also laid down his long-time traveling companion—a guitar—when it simply "wore out from too many trips on the road". He called this Alvarez Yari guitar, "Juniper". The instrument had almost taken on a personality of its own, constantly at the side of the singer, thrilling the hearts of the listeners. Over the years, many people have given John guitars, some of them beautifully handmade. Since then John Michael has played the world's finest guitars made by Ramirez, and Manuel Contreras II, donated for free, or for radically reduced prices to help the ministry. But there would be no replacement for dear old Juniper. John had learned that while family, loved ones, community members, even guitars, had coursed in and out of his life, one thing had remained through it all. The music.

In 1990 John would make a decision that would shake some of his friends and partners. He left Sparrow Records, growing more disillusioned with the direction of contemporary Christian music. While he held his friend and mentor, Billy Ray Hearn, in high esteem, he recognized that new values had replaced the spiritual ethic on which music ministry had been founded in a modern context. Now, he concluded, it all boiled down to money.

"In the early days of contemporary Christian music, it was clear there was a movement that was Spirit-driven. Suddenly, over a few short years, this industry had become money-driven," John asserts. "Money has to be considered, but it should never be primary. In early contemporary Christian music the message was clearly in the music. In recent years, executives are concerned with the bottom line. For example, it is widely understood throughout the contemporary Christian music world that if a new artist is to be signed, they must be young and good looking," John says. "The first generation of Contemporary Christian musicians usually left a successful career in secular music to use their music for pure ministry. Today, many music ministers seem to use their music to build a career, or as a doorway into secular music. It seemed to me that everything had been turned upside-down. At some point in my music ministry, it dawned on me that this industry was in trouble. I decided to leave."

The Master Musician / Sparrow

My relationship with Sparrow became increasingly strained the more Billy Ray Hearn stepped back from the helm, turning it over to his son, Bill. I had known Bill since before he was even a stock boy at Sparrow, when I used to stay in their house on visits to Los Angeles. As he took the helm, it was only natural that he would want to build a roster of artists that bore his stamp, just as his father had done.

This often put me at odds with the obvious direction of Sparrow and its reflection of Contemporary Christian Music. I was part of that enchanted first generation of musicians who sacrificed good secular careers for Christian music ministry. The newer generation of musicians and record execs wanted to move from music ministry to secular acceptance. Of course, this was all done in the name of evangelism, and there were legitimate possibilities for this expression, but it left the barn door wide open for money-motivated worldliness. It was only a matter of time before the ideological strain became too tense for either of us. Economics have always been realistically considered, but they were not as primary as they have become today.

I ended up calling Billy Ray, asking if it would be best for all involved if I just were to become disengaged from Sparrow. We had often discussed about taking the Troubadour imprint we had used on my product for years and making a Catholic branch of the label. Perhaps it would be helpful to start our own label now, I speculated. He said it would.

After calculations about recording company costs with the help of Phil Perkins, we launched Troubadour For The Lord recording with the Master Musician project. Zondervan published the book, which I wrote exclusively. It was a new beginning with a real sense of excitement at having greater spiritual and artistic control, but I was saddened to leave the company I had helped to build from the very start. That twinge of sadness stays with me even today, yet the fact that Sparrow would continue to distribute the new label retained a connection with the Sparrow family. I would be the last remaining original Sparrow artist to leave the nest. It was still a bit sad for all of us, but it is the only way to learn to fly.   ⏤ JMT

It was at this time that John remembered a dream God had given him years ago. In the dream he cut his hair and entered a big old house. Once inside he was shown all of the main rooms, and slowly found his way to all the back rooms and secret passageways. He got to know the house inside out. Then, he was

1990, during the recording of *Master Musician*, under the newly established record label, Troubadour for the Lord.

ushered through a doorway by a monk into the largest upstairs room. But all that he saw in the room was another stage ready and waiting! John was greatly disappointed. He awoke from the dream saying to the old monk," I want my hair back! They had preserved it for him, and hung it on the line!

While this dream seemed humorous, he knew it was largely fulfilled when he discovered that what was at the end of Christian music industry was another stage, and the need for the "long hair" of secular performance.

As his record sales peaked in the late '80s, John Michael Talbot expanded his outreach among Catholics and unchurched people in a dramatic way. This, he thought, merited the establishment of a new company: Troubadour For The Lord. The year was 1990. The music man who helped chart a new path was Phil Perkins, trusted friend, partner, and music arranger. Their first project was *Master Musician*, a recording–book package in which Talbot uses the music and the musician as metaphors for God and His people.

Master Musician and Meditation Series

We launched the new Label with a series of projects: The Master Musician, Meditations in the Spirit, *and* Meditations from Solitude. *The Master Musician was the project that distanced us from Sparrow, but it was a great concept and a good project to start with. But we immediately felt the absence of the big Sparrow machine that was usually behind us. It was a trade off. We got more artistic and spiritual freedom, but we lost the machinery of a big Gospel label behind our every move. We sold less, but profited more on the spiritual, artistic, and even the economic level.*

The Meditations in the Spirit *project gained momentum and sold very well. It was straight down the middle of the meditational scripture song style I am best known for. The*

> *songs were great and the performance continued to improve with each project. I also used a wonderful Ramirez guitar that had been donated to my ministry. All was back on track. "Veni Sancte Spiritus", Come Holy Spirit, became a standard in my concert repertoire.* Meditations from Solitude *is one of my absolute favorite recordings. It uses the great poetic lyrics from the monastic mystics of old, and puts them together with modern folk/classical songs, and wonderful orchestrations, and ethereal choral arrangements under my background vocal stacks. Though it is not one of the better selling projects, it continues to be one of my favorites to this day.* ⏤ JMT

Suddenly, new opportunities seemed to blow in like a fresh wind. John would plan collaborative recording projects with new artists, launch new ways of concert touring, and strategize new, creative communications with constituents, friends, and record buyers. The financial risks were high, matched only by the possibilities of a new level of spiritual payoff. On many occasions, Viola would say, "John, you know what the right thing is to do. You know God will show you the way." It was as though Viola and Jamie had joined their voices together: "Johnny, you tell them what your vision is, and let them decide if they want to be a part of it."

Spiritually emboldened, John launched out on a series of new projects that would require heavy doses of faith, prayer, and much hard work. For years he had barely toured, only doing occasional concerts. In 1995 he decided to schedule a series of concerts connected by bus routes. After all, he wondered, why fight the rigors of airline itineraries when a bus could preempt airline delays, and provide time and space for friends and touring partners, not to mention more time to pray, think, read, write and, yes, watch an occasional Star Wars movie!

The first time John and Viola rolled out on a bus concert tour, they knew they had found a wonderful alternative to frantic, punishing air travel. As they loped slowly along a sunny stretch of Florida freeway in a beautiful 40-foot fire engine red coach, piloted by an entertaining driver nicknamed Casper, John recalled with a shudder the days of his youth, crammed into a freezing van with the Mason Proffit band. Notably, this mode of travel is actually less costly than commercial flying, and much more suited to a life of prayer. Bus tours have now become a regular feature of John Michael Talbot's concert ministry.

John and Viola, always traveling together, have visited hundreds of towns and cities, sometimes accompanied by musicians or community members, powerfully touching the lives of hundreds of thousands of people. In nearly two decades, this author has attended hundreds of John Michael Talbot concert events. The faces of the listeners reflect a peaceful emotion, a beautiful blessing from the hand of God through His servant who still struggles occasionally with doubts about the effectiveness of his ministry. On occasion, John will quietly shrug, "maybe I should just give it all up. What I'm doing isn't radical enough. I think my best days of music may be over." It is startling to hear a man of such talent and accomplishments speak such words, particularly when so many have been so blessed for so long.

It just may be possible that many times more people outside America have been blessed through John Michael's extraordinary partnership with Mercy Corps. At most concerts there is a freewill offering prior to the intermission during which John explains the global humanitarian mission of this organization and why he is a part of it (for many years he has been the Chairman of Partners in Mercy, the monthly membership of Mercy Corps donors). Funds raised through his concert tours have opened doors of compassion in natural catastrophes, war zones, refugee camps, famines, and countless regions wracked by chronic poverty. One seasoned record business executive explained he had never in his life seen such a powerful partnership between a recording artist and a humanitarian organization. Many are alive and well today because of this extraordinary alliance. And because of the music.

John Michael Talbot's fascinating musical pilgrimage has led him into journeys of collaboration with other artists through concert tours and recordings, such as Phil Keaggy, Michael Card, Tony Melendez, Tom Booth, Barry McGuire, and big brother Terry. While briefly departing from his quiet, solo, signature albums to collaborate with other artists or experiment with more upbeat musical styles, John prefers his "quiet music".

John's meditational music was deemed important enough that a separate product line would be created—the Pathways Series. This sequential 6-CD project was composed of all instrumental tunes which John and the music industry call ambient music. Some call it "New Age" music, though those who create it do not always like this term. John Michael would say that in his meditational music—the space between the notes is as important as the notes. Once awakened to this reality, one can even hear the space within the notes. This is a lesson for learning to listen to all reality in life. John was pleased with the results of this project, having aimed for a special sound that would carry the meditational, Catholic, mystical tradition to, and even through, the listener. Pointing out that sin is inherently dissonant, John sees Christ reestablishing harmony, a process not only symbolized through the right kind of music, but also actualized through it.

Table of Plenty/Rich Mullins/LIFE TEEN

Table of Plenty was a collection of favorite Catholic contemporary worship songs from the twenty or so years since Vatican II. We joined forces with Oregon Catholic Press, the largest publisher of Catholic music in the United States, and owner of most of the copyrights. It became one of my bigger releases of the past ten years.

In the collection we tried to branch out into some World Music sounds with creative integrations of old and new, and also used some more contemporary treatments to augment my standard style. It only made sense that we would take some well-known Catholic musicians on the Table of Plenty Tour. We invited Tom Booth from the LIFE TEEN program, who I've known since the earliest days of that movement, and Tony Melendez, the well-known performer who, born without arms, plays guitar with his feet.

We were enthusiastically received as we toured across America in four touring legs over a one-and a half-year period. The musical combination blended my meditational music with the upbeat style of Tony, and the contemporary worship songs of Tom Booth. It also allowed me to do some of my more contemporary songs in concert with the others accompanying me. After years of performing entire concerts by myself, this was a pleasant change.

During the last leg of that tour we received the tragic news that Rich Mullins had just been killed in a traffic accident. Tom was closest to him, and immediately dropped to his knees and tearfully prayed in the entryway of the church. Rich was ready to be Confirmed as a Catholic in just a few weeks in Mesa Arizona at St. Timothy's, the home church of LIFE TEEN.

I didn't know Rich well. He had come to the monastery a couple of times seeking direction from God in a place dedicated to prayer. He looked like a man who was searching for something, but didn't know what it was. He spoke of the Church, but wasn't convinced. He loved St. Francis, but wasn't sure about Catholic Franciscans. We did not intrude on his retreat, but were simply available for any questions he might have, *much as the Friars had once done for me. Since his death, some have tried to minimize his Catholic and Franciscan tendencies. They do a disservice to Rich by doing so. But I have maintained contact through some of his Kid Brothers of St. Franck band members like Eric Hauk on cello, who has gone out on the road with me in the chamber group.*

I knew Fr. Dale, the founder of LIFE TEEN, when he was a Deacon at St. Jerome's on the north side of Phoenix. After he was ordained and assigned to St. Tim's I began to work with the parish in citywide concerts and in parish missions. LIFE TEEN was originally the youth program only at St. Tim's, but when it grew into some 1100 young people at every Sunday evening Liturgy, other parishes began to take notice. Centered on Jesus, the Eucharist, and the Church, LIFE TEEN actively involves the parish priest, a good music group, and Life Night where an energetic Mass is followed by small group sharing. Though criticized by some on various points, LIFE TEEN enjoys the support of the Pope and the Bishops, and has spread to over 600 parishes nationwide, and is the most on fire youth program I have seen in the Church in America today. — JMT

Interestingly, not many Christians have ventured into musical styles that try to speak the unspeakable beyond words, ideas, or forms. This would be called contemplative music. Christian Contemporary Music has remained primarily involved with using the popular styles of the secular west to reach the people of the west. Catholic Music has remained primarily liturgical. But John Michael would point out that the mystical and contemplative aspect of the full Catholic Christian tradition is not being adequately reflected in its music. Both his instrumental and vocal music help to fill this present void, and point the way for others to go in this direction.

This promotional photo was taken in 1997 for the *Table of Plenty* album.

Simple Heart / Terry & Barry

After the more radical departures from my traditional sound with Cave of the Heart *and the* Pathways *instrumental series, we came out with two recordings that were "in the pocket" of the sound that listeners loved most. These are the* Simple Heart *and* Wisdom *recordings.*

Simple Heart *is a collection of new meditational scripture and Catholic prayer songs. I toured this project across the country with my brother Terry, and longtime friend Barry*

McGuire. They had already been part of the larger team for the previous Cave of the Heart *tour. Terry and Barry would get the audience singing, clapping, tapping their toes, stomping their feet, and just plain laughing. Then I would take the stage and guide the audience through a quieter worship experience with meditational music and prayer. The result was a well-rounded evening.*

It was also personally satisfying for me. Terry was the one who taught me how to sing and play. Barry is the one who taught me how to sing for God. When I was still new to Christian music I was trying all of my secular skills to reach the audience. Barry gave me advice that would change my life. Touring with Terry and Barry will remain one of my greatest memories of touring. ⌐ JMT

John Michael Talbot in 2001, the promotional photo for *Simple Heart*.

John Michael designs his concerts in such a way that his unique musical style and special song sequence moves the listener into retreat mode. He likes to take the open, thoughtful participant on a scriptural journey from ancient to contemporary, lifting the willing soul to new heights of prayerful worship. As stated earlier, John believes even the silence between musical notes carries meaning and significance. "We know that Jesus was the Incarnate Word. We also know He was not always speaking, therefore, the Word with all its meaning persists even in that silent space," he says.

It is important to note that the environment of the Little Portion Hermitage monastery finds its way into the music, not only because of John's prayerful attitude as he writes the songs, but also because he now records in a mini-studio he constructed in his small hermitage. The idea began when a recording project requiring singing by community members necessitated the presence of a mobile sound studio. John began to gradually acquire the equipment needed to record albums beginning with the purchase of two digital studio workstations and gradually building a computer-based sound studio. His first recording to emerge from the monastery studio was *Table of Plenty*.

1997 was a watershed year for John Michael's commitment to music ministry through the founding of the Catholic Association of Musicians. Not only was the *Table of Plenty* album enthusiastically received, the tour by the same name, which included Catholic recording artists Tom Booth and Tony Melendez, was a smashing success as they toured throughout the country to critical acclaim.

After John's initial success in Christian music, he was besieged with demo tapes and letters from aspiring Catholic artists who wanted to have success in ministry themselves. He had always been happy to give encouraging words to others, but soon he realized that he had a responsibility to assist Catholic contemporary musicians in a tangible way. John's advisors had warned him against starting a new Catholic label. First, the so-called Catholic market was uncharted. Many strong Protestant record companies had tried unsuccessfully to reach Catholics. Second, Catholic artists were still undeveloped compared to their Contemporary Christian Music counterparts. Third, starting a record label was a very expensive prospect, and was likened by many to throwing hard earned capital into a financial black hole.

Then one night he was inspired to help in a totally different way. He would start an association of artists and companies not to establish record deals, but to provide a network for spiritual support, artistic cooperation, dialogue, and business education that would benefit all. He shared the idea with those same advisors, and got unanimous support. He then received positive input from the Brothers and Sisters of Charity community, and the bishop.

The Catholic Association of Musicians, or CAM, was born. The first meeting was a huge success, because most of the artists had never had the chance to meet each other in person, and many lasting personal and professional relationships were forged.

Greg Walton performs during a trade show with the Catholic Association of Musicians, founded by John Michael in 1996 to assist aspiring Catholic artists.

Next, CAM put together a set of statutes that stated its purpose, and placed itself under the guidance of the General Council of the Brothers and Sisters of Charity, which also placed them under the Church. CAM's own leadership council was elected, including a representative for Oregon Catholic Press, Phil Perkins, and John Michael.

In its first six years, CAM has brought in presenters chosen from the very best of the Catholic, early CCM, and CBA music industry to speak at its annual conference. CAM members have had the opportunity to get up close and personal with industry leaders who would normally be encountered only at some distance in a larger convention setting.

Mike Card, Phil Keaggy, Barry McGuire and Terry Talbot, Billy Ray Hearn, Phil Perkins, Steve Griffin and leaders from Word and Hosanna/Integrity have all shared from their wealth of experience in Christian Contemporary Music. Catholic leaders like Dave Island from Oregon Catholic Press, Tom Booth from LIFE TEEN, Tony Melendez and his brother Jose, Dana Scallon, and many more have shared their Catholic perspective. The wealth of many lifetimes has been shared as a gift with CAM members.

By design, CAM's annual conference has been kept in a simple retreat setting at Little Portion's retreat center. John feels that this preserves CAM's priorities of spirituality, artistry, and economy, in that order. Most who have come to these CAM gatherings from CCM say that the Spirit at work with these artists feels like the early days of Jesus Music. They say that it is like a breath of fresh air – like the wind of the Spirit.

"According to my sources," says John, "Jesus Music and CCM first got their directions from Catholic Folk Mass musicians." The Baptists didn't know how to bring contemporary music into the traditional church, so they asked the Catholics who were already making progress in that direction. The Baptists, seeing the power of popular styles of music, quickly developed a non-liturgical use of music as a tool for evangelism, while Catholics continued their growth at a slower rate, due to the checks and balances of the Bishops in liturgical music.

Since the advent of John Paul II's World Youth Days, reaching Catholic young people has taken on a special urgency. Music is a vital tool in reaching the younger generation through a cultural language to which they can relate. Today the Catholic Church is better prepared for the use of contemporary music in a suitable way, both during liturgy, and outside of liturgy at other gatherings.

CAM continues as a ministry of the Brothers and Sisters of Charity. Its refreshing blend of Catholic artists in all musical styles and ecumenical veteran mentors has become an inspiring movement. John hopes that CAM will one day stand as an autonomous organization.

In concert in December 2001 at the Eureka Springs Auditorium.

Wisdom & the Wisdom Tour

I had written the songs for the Wisdom *album years before, some as far back as* Heart of the Shepherd. *I always had a special place in my heart for these songs. I had even invited Mike Card to come in and sing. We actually began* Wisdom *before the* Brother to Brother *project. We used Ron Huff as our primary orchestrator. He is considered one of the best in the country and is a wonderful human being to be around. Also, we got Billy Ray to come out of retirement and drop by the studio on the orchestra sessions. It was like old times. The songs came out as a lovely slice of musical art. I am very pleased with that project.*

In late 2001 and early 2002 we embarked on one of the more difficult, and most timely, tours of my career; the Wisdom *Tour. It came on the heels of the terrorist tragedies of September 11. The* Wisdom *recording had been released in September, and the tour embarked soon after, including a parish in New York City just blocks from ground zero. The crises in the Holy Land heated up just prior to Holy Week of 2002, as did the sexual scandals within the Roman Catholic Church. All of these events hit close to home for me, because I knew people closely involved in various pastoral aspects of each area. It was a time of great emotional turmoil and instability for the faithful of America and the Catholic Church in America. The recording and the Tour could not have come at a worse, or a better time.*

The tour netted mixed results, with crowds both large and small. Some were disheartened with anything remotely religious or even spiritual. Others needed it more than ever before. But the ministry was truly great everywhere we visited. City after city, and parish after parish, the gentle music seemed to soak into the troubled souls of thousands as we tried to bring the healing calm of the reassuring faith, hope, and charity of

> *God in a way beyond words. It seemed to bring a power beyond anything that can be manipulated through empty human effort alone.*
>
> *I was profoundly grateful to be invited in to parishes across America at this time. I was truly stunned and humbled night after night at the way in which the Lord works when all human answers seem to pale in comparison to the crises we face. In this time it is enormously clear that salvation comes from God and God alone through Christ.* ⟶ JMT

In 2001 John Michael Talbot celebrated 25 years of Christian music with 45 albums to his credit, 15 books, numerous awards and a ministry outreach that spans the globe. In 2003 he celebrates an equally important anniversary: his silver anniversary as a Catholic, and consecrated life in community.

EMI Christian Records presents John Michael an award in recognition of his 25th year of Christian music ministry at the Christian Booksellers' Convention in 2001.

The achievements have been, in the words of one journalist, "remarkable". Through it all John continues to ask the question, "Have I really done what God wants me to do?" There is, at times, a kind of holy restlessness that seizes this man's soul that hearkens back through the centuries in the life of the little man from Assisi: St. Francis. A clear mark of St. Francis' mission was itinerancy—wandering in a spirit of radical obedience blown by the wind of the Holy Spirit in radical abandonment to Divine Providence. "I still haven't done enough of it," John quietly reflects, almost as if touched by a slight shade of guilt, "but it is coming." These were John's words in the mid '90s, and he was right. The itinerant ministry of the Brothers and Sisters of Charity based at The Little Portion Hermitage began to blossom in new ways.

The 2001 National Gathering of the Brothers and Sisters of Charity, Monastic and Domestic Members.

John Michael with daughter Amy, her husband, Jonathan, and John's grandson, Isaac.

The Joy of Music Ministry/
Come to the Quiet book

In recent years I have been more active as a writer, completing two books for my 25-year celebration of ministry in 2001, and 25 years as a Catholic in 2003. The books are The Joy of Music Ministry *and* Come to the Quiet. *Each book comes from my experience as a Catholic Christian musician, monastic leader and teacher.*

Both books were written pretty easily in their first drafts. For The Joy of Music Ministry, *I sat back and let the words flow.* Come to the Quiet, *which is about Christian meditation, came pretty much the same way, though its subject matter was a bit deeper by its nature. Each book is related to the other, because my music flows from prayer, and my prayer overflows into teaching and music ministry.*

The Joy of Music Ministry *begins with a section of the spiritual reordering of our spirit, soul, and body in Christ to rediscover the music of God within us. It then reaches out by looking at the official teaching of the Church, and the Scriptures, and concludes with the analogy of the orchestra or music group to encourage living and making music in the Church.* Come to the Quiet *also establishes the right ordering of spirit, soul, and body through a teaching on meditation and contemplative prayer in the Christian east and west. It concludes by meeting the challenge of the rise in popularity of eastern meditation methods through a fitting complement and completion of them all in Christ and the Church.*

Both books are being received well in their oral teaching form, and in writing. LIFE TEEN has used The Joy of Music Ministry *as a teaching for all of their musicians across the country.*

— JMT

Teaching at a Catholic conference in 2001.

It is noteworthy to mention two scriptures given to John Michael early on to describe his music ministry. The first is most direct. Ezekiel 33:32 says, "For them you are only a ballad singer, with a pleasant voice and a clever touch. They listen to your words, but will not obey them. But when it comes—and it is surely coming—they shall know that there was a prophet among them." Despite the gentle nature of John's music, many call it prophetic concerning the radical nature of its actual content. A glance back through this book confirms that reality. Like Jesus whom he follows, John Michael's music brings the challenge of a full gospel reality to the serious listener. This can be both comforting, and disturbing.

The second scripture is from Revelation 11 concerning the two witnesses who prophesy in sackcloth. Their words are hard for people to bear, so they are executed "in Jerusalem." The people rejoice at their death, but God takes them up to heaven. Likewise, John Michael's lifestyle and teaching ministry have brought comfort to millions, but still make some uncomfortable. He has confronted typical western lifestyles. Some have sought to discredit, or silence John through the years, but God continues to raise him up despite the sometimes-heated opposition.

There is one thing that remains as the enduring component, indeed, the heartbeat of John Michael Talbot's multi-faceted mission that has stretched over the decades, and around the world.

It is the music of God.

The music lives.

Epilogue

~

This story of John Michael Talbot's journey is not a comprehensive life history. It would be more accurate to say that this book has been about the Gospel, using John's pilgrimage to cast it in modern terms. John would insist that the crux of this story is more the exemplary life of Saint Francis of Assisi, St Antony of the Desert, or St. Benedict of Nursia, and the saints of monasticism in general, than it is his own life. However, these monastic saints undoubtedly defer and point to Christ, claiming that only He can be our supreme model for faith. Nonetheless, there are elements in the life of this modern-day troubadour that make him particularly relevant to our age.

It is apparent that God placed an unusual call on John's life. It is perhaps more true to say, however, that all of us have a unique call of God upon us, but we sometimes fail to recognize the call or to be fully obedient to it. John's story compels us all to examine ourselves in order to seek out those abilities and gifts that uniquely mark us for our life's work.

John's life also speaks to us of conversion—a transforming, awakening process whereby we acknowledge the lordship of Christ and inaugurate a lifelong movement toward him, with all its inevitable ups and downs.

It is only in coming to know God that we can, in turn, make Him known. We become the image of Christ in a lost world. It is in this context that John's integrated monastic lifestyle communicates so much: voluntary poverty in the face of addictive consumerism, chastity in the face of rampant promiscuity, obedience in the face of self centered individualism. They embrace silence in a society of endless words and information, but really communicate rarely, solitude in the face of the crowded cities that tend to isolate rather than bring together in community. Lastly, they represent love of God and humanity in a world where violence is spreading and God is rarely acknowledged.

Over the years John Michael Talbot has accomplished a great deal. His music has bridged Catholic and non Catholic Christians. The community he founded has brought integrations in a historic proportion—the charismatic and the contemplative, the liturgical and the spontaneous, the hermetical lifestyle with that of the traditional monastic community. The Franciscan and the Benedictine, Camaldolese, Carthusian and Cistercian, as well as the Carmelite, Augustinian, and other expressions of consecrated life can be seen in the life of the Bothers and Sisters of Charity. States of life, such as celibate, single, family monastic, and domestic, are brought together in a gospel way that is traditional, yet progressively forward-looking. The community has also integrated all major faith traditions of the world from a Christian base, and all religious and monastic expressions from a Franciscan base. Yet, the community is not Franciscan, but is a child born of its' Franciscan mother that constitutes a child that is unique and new.

John's music itself has broken down many barriers where words alone have proven ineffective. He has bridged various styles through contemporary, classical, folk, and meditational styles. Though best known for his meditational style, he has integrated ancient and modern styles long before world music, or new age music, were an established part of our musical language. Of course, with Mason Proffit John Michael was a groundbreaker with the Country Rock style that became the foundation for modern country music. As a soloist he was also on the ground floor of what would later be called Christian Contemporary Music. It is his music, and the mysterious and intimate work of God on individual human hearts and lives that remain the most stunning fruit of John's life of faith. Countless letters, e-mails, and phone calls attest to the powerful way God works through John Michael's simple music. Those who experienced conversion to God, Jesus Christ, the Catholic Church, and more personal stories of redemption from lives of desperation and death, continue to be the fruit of his music and books. Beyond the more obvious use of his music during Eucharist, people have been baptized and confirmed to the accompaniment of his music, as well as proposals, marriages, conceptions, ordinations, anointing for the sick, penances, and even passing into the next life. All of these things represent a work of grace through his simple music that is truly beyond description. It is a matter of God's ineffable gift of love through Jesus Christ. John Michael and the community he founded continue in awe of the grace of God that works through all of us who simply submit our gifts and talents to God.

This is perhaps the greatest message of any testimony like John Michael Talbot's. Ultimately it is not John Michael, or any other Christian celebrity or example, which are the point of these stories. It is you and I. It is the regular follower of Christ who is the real subject of these stories. John Michael simply uses the gifts that God gave him for God's glory, nothing more, nothing less. This is something to which we are all called in Christ and His Church. In this no one is more important than any other. No story is more profound than any other. There is no Jew or Gentile, male or female, slave or free.

In spite of his success in furthering his spiritual ideals, he feels he still falls far short. "Just look at Francis's life and see what was accomplished," he says. "By the end of his ministry there were hundreds of thousands of Franciscans who made deep, life-changing faith commitments to live a penitential Gospel life. This was all done without television, radio, or a Christian media network. This was accomplished one to one, person-to-person, at the street level. Like the great Christian evangelists of history and modern times, it included the large crowds that came to hear him speak, or to be graced by his healing touch from Jesus. We're talking about a genuine and revolutionary spiritual movement of love rooted in prayer. I find this tremendously challenging as we continue to build our community.

"Or take the example of St. Romuald, the founder of the Camaldolese Hermits and Monks. It is said that he reformed a dizzying number of monasteries during his religious vocation. This means he only stayed a short time in each monastery, reforming them by example and the establishment of a Prior or Abbot to keep things going. Then he would move on. He also spent years at a time in strict solitude in a hermitage.

I have been given so much, but have accomplished so much less. Part of this is because we live in different times. Joining a monastery was a very acceptable social choice in those days. In some ways it was a step 'up' the social ladder. Plus, a lifetime vocational commitment was the norm, not the exception. Today this is not the case. Living in a secluded hermitage for life is hard to sell to an upwardly mobile, typically transient American, Catholic Christian or not."

On an even more expansive level, the Catholic Church in itself has been the object of many of John's hopes and prayers. He represents a whole new generation of Catholic converts from the Evangelical and Jesus Movement expressions of faith. They bring new blood and zealous vitality, challenging those with ready hearts and open minds to renewal and appropriate reform. He builds his case for the future upon the solid foundation of long-established tradition and devotion found in the church itself. It is part of John's call to present the truths of the faith in new ways, prophetically calling the church to reexamine itself in light of its own tenets.

"The Catholic Church has all of the gifts within her possession, but they are often left on the shelf of the spiritual pantry, and have not been actively used. Other churches and ecclesial communities also have some of these gifts on their shelves, but they use them very well. We Catholics would be foolish not to work with other expressions of Christianity and religion in order to find out how to actively use these gifts ourselves."

John Michael has worked toward the goal of Christian unity and interfaith cooperation throughout his life. Also, such problems of our day as world hunger and peace have always occupied important places within Catholicism, and these are areas to which John and his community seek to address.

Until such time as his visions of Christian unity and renewal, and interfaith cooperation and respect have been realized, John and Viola, along with the Brothers and Sisters of Charity, will persist in their call to simplicity and prayer. "We root ourselves in mystical union with Christ. We remain sensitive to the workings and the leading of the Spirit of God in our lives. If we do these things and listen in the stillness of our own spirits, we will be able to hear His words of guidance. And we will go where He leads us."

John Michael concludes, "I have had the privilege of sharing one particular song with the President, the Pope, and Mother Teresa. It is the Peace Prayer of St. Francis. This simple prayer has comforted, inspired, empowered and energized the community and followers through the years. I hope its lyric is helpful and appropriate. But, may we not just pray this prayer, but live it as well."

Lord, make me an instrument of your peace.
Where there is hatred, let me sow love.
Where there is injury, pardon.
Where there is doubt, faith.
Where there is despair, hope.
Where there is darkness, light.
Where there is sadness, joy.

O Divine Master, grant that I may not so much seek
To be consoled, as to console,
To be understood, as to understand,
To be loved, as to love.

For it is in giving, that we receive,
It is in pardoning, that we are pardoned.
It is in dying, that we are born to eternal life.

Legacy

In recent years I have had the pleasure of looking out over our monastic Motherhouse for the Brothers and Sisters of Charity at Little Portion Hermitage, and seeing the dream and vision God gave me over 30 years ago slowly being fulfilled. It is not yet perfect, but it is substantive. This is a graphic lesson for me in patience and perseverance, neither of which has come easily. It has taken 30 years of being obedient to God one day at a time to fulfill. The same is true for any of our dreams and visions. We must have patience, and we must persevere. Only then are they realized in God's time and way.

St. John of the Cross once wrote that when we stand before God, the Eternal, we would only be asked one question: How well have you loved? None of our religious intellectual, ministry, or institutional accomplishments will mean much at that moment in Eternity and Infinity. Ultimately, it is not what we accomplish in God's name that is important. It is knowing the reality of God that is really important in the Eternal and Infinite value of even spiritual things.

Years ago in interviews when questioned about the future I would say that my greatest goal is to simply "go deeper into the sacred wounds of Christ." All else flows almost spontaneously from that one Reality. Today I believe that more than ever. But instead of it being some kind of romantic mystical notion, it is realized in the ordinary struggles and pains of life. It is there that we find the lasting comfort and strength of God in Christ. This is, without question, the most important thing in my life as I look back over the past 25 years, and forward to however long God wants me to live.

As to legacies, there have been two prophecies given to me regarding our community. The first is of a great multitude of people streaming into our monastic valley as a place of refuge during a time of great tribulation in the west. The other is of me walking totally alone through a deserted Hermitage. In their own way both are true, have been fulfilled, and have yet to be fulfilled. We have seen people stream into this place from all across our country, and from around the world. We have also seen the many leave.

Personally, I have yet to radically fulfill the vision of walking on foot from parish to parish in itinerant mendicancy. Traditionally, this occurs only after a greater time in extended solitude. Viola and I will always be the spiritual Father and Mother of this community, but we have both desired to retire to a little hermitage away from the active life of the monastery, which many abbots and abbesses in the Christian East and Far East have traditionally done. Perhaps we will get to fulfill that aspect of the call someday.

I have nothing much to share, and everything to share. I must be truly happy with obscurity in order for God to accomplish anything of external worth and notice through me, or anyone else.

If just one person out of all who have heard the music, read the books, joined the Church, or come to the community authentically grasps and receives the transmission of the spirit of my teaching in the Spirit of Jesus, I will have considered my life a success. It could be in my lifetime. It could be much later. That ultimate teaching is the complete letting go of the old person, inside and out, through the dying of Jesus, so that we might awaken to His resurrection as a whole new person and way of living in Christ. That is really all that a monastery, or the Church for that matter, is ultimately here on earth for.

In this light I have had to let go of even the vision and the community God showed me 25 years ago. I have had to find value in this life in something far more interior and personal than external accomplishment.

I am reminded of little brother Charles De Foucault. He spent a lifetime founding a new community in northern Africa to reach those still practicing the old folk religions of the region. Despite a lifetime of struggle, sacrifice, and pain, not one person ever joined him. There was not one convert to Christianity, and not one person who joined his new community. One day some robbers came by his lone hermitage thinking that he was a French spy. When they discovered that there was no booty stashed in his hermitage they shot Charles through the head. His life was over in an instant. Some would say that he wasted his life.

Years later someone was walking through that same desert, and kicked up something in the sand with the toe of their boot. It was Brother Charles' journal. In it they read about the vision God had given him about a new community. They took the journal, and little Brother Charles' vision was made a reality. Today The Little Brothers and Sisters of Jesus, and the Gospel constitute five new communities in the Church. Two are contemplative, and two are active. There are also lay people associated with the communities.

Today Charles De Foucault stands as an example of hope for me, and others who have been given a vision from God in these most perilous times for the Church in the west. I can often feel very discouraged when the vision is not realized in the time or way that I thought that it would. Charles stands as an example that not one moment, not one day, and certainly not one life of sacrifice for God will go without accomplishing the will of God.

It is an example to me that none of it is in vain.

~ JMT

Appendix

JOHN MICHAEL TALBOT DISCOGRAPHY AND BOOK LIST

ALBUMS

2003 · Signatures
2001 · Wisdom
2000 · Simple Heart
1999 · Cave of the Heart
1998 · Spirit Pathways
1998 · Quiet Pathways
1998 · Pathways to Wisdom
1998 · Pathways to Solitude
1998 · Pathways of the Shepherd
1998 · Hidden Pathways
1997 · Table of Plenty
1996 · Troubadour for the Lord
1996 · Our Blessing Cup
1996 · Brother to Brother
1995 · The Talbot Brothers Collection
1995 · The John Michael Talbot Collection
1995 · Chant from the Hermitage
1994 · Meditations from Solitude
1993 · Meditations in the Spirit
1992 · The Master Musician
1990 · The Birth of Jesus
1990 · Hiding Place
1990 · Come Worship the Lord Vol. 2
1990 · Come Worship the Lord Vol. 1
1989 · The Lover and the Beloved
1989 · Master Collection

1988 · The Regathering
1987 · Quiet Reflections
1987 · Heart of the Shepherd
1986 · Empty Canvas
1986 · Be Exalted
1985 · The Quiet
1985 · Songs For Worship Vol. 2
1984 · The God of Life
1983 · No Longer Strangers
1982 · Songs For Worship Vol. 1
1982 · Light Eternal
1981 · Troubadour of the Great King
1981 · For the Bride
1980 · The Painter
1980 · Come to the Quiet
1980 · Beginnings / The Early Years
1979 · The Lord's Supper
1977 · The New Earth
1976 · John Michael Talbot
1972 · Reborn (The Talbot Brothers)

BOOKS
2003 · Signatures
2002 · Come to the Quiet — Christian Meditation
2001 · The Joy of Music Ministry
1999 · The Music of Creation
1997 · The Lessons of St. Francis
1994 · Meditations from Solitude
1992 · The Master Musician
1991 · A Passion for God
1991 · Blessings
1989 · Simplicity with Dan O'Neill
1989 · Hermitage
1988 · Regathering Power
1987 · Reflections on the Gospels Vol. 2
1986 · Reflections on the Gospels Vol. 1
1985 · The Lover and the Beloved
1984 · The Fire of God
1984 · Changes

SONGBOOKS
1999 · One Faith
1998 · Light Eternal
1997 · The Lord's Supper
1995 · Chant From The Hermitage
1995 · Our Blessing Cup
1991 · Come Worship The Lord
1987 · Praise, Prayer, & Worship
1985 · Songs For Worship
1983 · The Songs of John Michael Talbot Vol. II
1980 · The Songs of John Michael Talbot Vol. I

VIDEOS
2001 — Live In Concert
Quiet Reflections
Franciscan Holy Ground
Pathways to Catholic Christianity
Fire of God Rekindled
New Life through the Cross
Audio Teaching
Gifts of the Holy Spirit

Footnotes

Chapter 5

1 By John Michael Talbot from the album *The Talbot Brothers: Reborn*. 1974 Warner Brothers Records, 1976 Sparrow Records International, published by Flying Arrow Publishing (ASCAP).

2 G.K. Chesterton, *Orthodoxy* (New York: Doubleday, 1959), p. 48.

Chapter 6

1 Matthew 6:16.

2 G.K. Chesterton, *Orthodoxy* (New York: Doubleday, 1959), p. 48.

3 John 6:41–60.

4 Chesterton, op.cit.,p.83.

Chapter 7

1 Karl Adam, *The Spirit of Catholicism* (New York: Doubleday, 1954),p.241.

2 Matthew 19:24.

3 Luke 9:3.

4 Matthew 10:38.

5 Thomas Merton, *The Silent Life* (New York: Farrar, Straus and Giroux, 1957), p.47.

6 Luke 11:9.

7 G.K. Chesterton, *Orthodoxy*, p. 29.

8 John Michael Talbot, S.F.O., *The Regathering* (Indianapolis: The Little Portion House of Prayer, 1981).

Chapter 9

1 John Michael Talbot, S.F.O., "Franciscan Community in Today's World" (Alverna, Indianapolis: The Little Portion House of Prayer, 1980).

2 John Michael Talbot, S.F.O., "Secular Franciscan Houses of Prayer" (Alverna, Indianapolis: The Little Portion House of Prayer, 1980). Topics covered include purpose, prayer, study, conversion of manners, apostolic service, poverty, property, clothing, food, recreation, the hermitage, mendicancy, covenant promises, government.

3 The offices are liturgical prayers follow sequentially through a breviary, or prayer book, based upon the church calendar. This is standard practice in varying formats in all Catholic religious communities.

4 The Byzantine crucifix at the ruins of the church of San Damiano (Saint Damien) is said to have miraculously spoken to Saint Francis, urging him to rebuild the church.

5 By Duane W.H. Arnold, M.A., and C. George Fry, Ph.D., D.Min.

Chapter 10

1 II Kings 22–23.

2 St. Francis of Assisi, Writings and Early Biographies: English Omnibus of Sources for the Life of St. Francis, edited by Marion A. Habig (Chicago: Franciscan Herald Press, 1973), pp. 1413–14.

3 Ibid., p. 1898.